Donna Tartt's
The Secret History

CONTINUUM CONTEMPORARIES

Also available in this series

Forthcoming in this series

· **DONNA TARTT'S**

The Secret History

A READER'S GUIDE

TRACY HARGREAVES

CONTINUUM | NEW YORK | LONDON

2001

The Continuum International Publishing Group Inc
370 Lexington Avenue, New York, NY 10017

The Continuum International Publishing Group Ltd
The Tower Building, 11 York Road, London SE1 7NX

Printed in the United States of America

Library of Congress Cataloging-in-Publication Data

Hargreaves, Tracy.
    Donna Tartt's The secret history : a reader's guide / Tracy Hargreaves.
        p. cm. — (Continuum contemporaries)
    Includes bibliographical references.
    ISBN 0-8264-5320-1 (pbk. : alk. paper)
    I. Tartt, Donna. Secret history. 2. College stories, American—History
and criticism.   I. Title.   II. Series.

PS3570.A657 S4 2001
813'.54—dc21   2001032433

Contents

1

The Novelist

Donna Tartt was born in Greenwood, Mississippi in 1963, the eldest of two daughters born to Don and Taylor Tartt. Tartt has described her father (a local politician) as "dashing but feckless," and her mother, as "skittish, immature," a woman still referred to by her family as Baby, but regarded by Tartt as graceful, light-hearted, affectionate and with a real affinity for the childlike world of her young daughter.[1] Her mother's family, that "dear old bad old Boushé family" acknowledged "most of all" in *The Secret History*, had long established roots in Greenwood, though Tartt herself was raised in nearby Grenada.

Grenada has been described as a listless place of no great distinction, and such details have inevitably prompted speculation that Tartt drew from her own life in transporting her narrator, Richard Papen, from his cheerless origins in "Plano, California" to the enchantment of Hampden. She is circumspect about her private life; James Kaplan suggests that she is "highly guarded (to say the least) about any relationship between the novel and her own life."[2] It's too crude to suggest that Tartt dropped bits of her life into her fiction, and while there *are* similarities, they take us nowhere, critically or imaginatively, beyond a recognition of the coincidence.

And yet the details that she does tell about herself are revealing. Her earliest interviews suggest a determination to control or fashion a version of her life as a writer's life in the making. Hers, as she tells it, was influenced by an allegiance to early nineteenth century and Victorian writers, filtered through the sensibilities of three generations of her Mississippian family. She was raised in her infancy by an extended and, by her own account, loving family of great-aunts and great-grandparents, commenting, but choosing not to elaborate, that "my parents were neither able nor inclined to take much of an interest in my early upbringing." ("Sleepytown, 1992") Her earliest memories, then, come from the "old house on Commerce Street", in which she was fussed and worried over by aged aunts and a great-grandfather who remained convinced that his sickly granddaughter would not survive during the feverish nights of her childhood illnesses. Only when her upwardly mobile parents hired a maid and seemed better able to cope with her did Tartt return to them, although she was still visited daily by this entourage, who claimed that her mother, Taylor, wasn't "any better mother than a cat", a remark that, when innocently repeated to her by her daughter, she understandably found upsetting.

Absent parents and dysfunctional and alternative family structures are the norm in *The Secret History* which is replete with orphans and abandoned and unloved children, who in early adulthood are still seeking strong paternal figures (like Julian) and establishing close familial bonds with each other. They end up controlled and imprisoned in an impotent stalemate, locked between a child-adult existence, determined by the control (benign and otherwise) of older family members (the fates of Camilla and Francis), or, as is the case with Richard, apparently destined for an isolated existence.

Whereas academic criticism has looked to Classical Greek and Latin in order to appraise her work, the first swath of book reviews generally dismissed her knowledge of Classics and American, English, and European literature as an insubstantial pose. Bret Easton Ellis's influence, though often cited, is really discernible only in that group of "Generation X" campus characters that people Hampden, like Cloke and Judy. Some critics have pointed to films like Hitchcock's *Rope* (based on Patrick Hamilton's play of the same name) as an influence, in which two arrogant students, Brandon Shaw and Philip Morgan, murder a classmate, put his body in a trunk, and then invite his family and friends round for dinner, using the trunk as a table; their subsequent nervous guilt eventually gives them away. Also cited as influences have been examples of America's privileged and affluent youth who consider themselves above the law, like Erik and Lyle Menendez who murdered their parents, fearing they were about to be disinherited. Or again, Leopold and Loeb, the Chicago students who in 1924 murdered and kidnapped the 14-year-old Robert Frank because they wanted to commit the perfect crime. But Henry, after all, doesn't kill just to see if he can get away with it since the first murder is accidental, the second done for self-interest.

Books have really seemed to animate Tartt throughout her life, and the narrative she fashions about herself speaks to an ambition, desire and identity formed through literature, although as a writer she also seems to have inherited some of the idiosyncratic traits of her elderly relatives "who possessed a kind of effusive, elegiac fatalism which expressed itself in long gloomy visits to the cemetery and melancholy ruminations on the vanity of human wishes" (as fitting an epigraph as any for the book that Tartt would go on to write). ("Sleepytown, 1992")

By her own account, she was a precocious child. At Miss Doty's Kindergarten for Girls she announced that she "should like to be an ar-chae-ologist" when she grew up. She attended Miss Kirk's Academy, but was at school for "no more than three days a week and usually I didn't stay the whole day."[3] Poor attendance was a consequence of poor health (rather than any more skittish tendencies) between the ages of five and seven. In one interview she claimed to spend this time reading books in bed (just as Henry does in *The Secret History*, p. 51). But in another memoir she recalled "long, drugged afternoons in bed", sleepy with codeine and enjoying a "languorous undersea existence" in which the surreal landscape of her imagination began to evolve and she imagined herself flying with Peter Pan, like an incipient De Quincey, woozy on childhood medicines. Everything suggested something else: the glow from the gas heater inspired her to see Tom and Huck's campfire; a rattling truck made her think of dinosaurs, and the neighborhood trees were like Jurassic tree-ferns. At least, this is how Tartt recalled her childhood back in 1992. By the end of the decade, she remembered differently that it was her boredom that had inspired her as a writer: "I spent a lot of time alone when I was a child—a lot of unstructured time, without organized activities or other children to play with—and on an almost daily basis I sank into crashing, absolutely stupendous boredoms: lying on the floor and staring in a daze at the leg of a chair, or the quilted diamond pattern of my toybox, or something like that, for hours on end."[4] But it was while her mind was thus inactive that stories and characters began to come to her.

Her desire to be an archaeologist was fostered by reading a book (given to her by her grandmother) about Heinrich Schliemann, the Victorian archaeologist and classicist who re-discovered Troy and Mycenae. And concomitant with this early interest in classicism was a liking for Victorian writers, in particular Charles Dickens. She was once asked who she would be if she were a character in fiction, and replied that she would be a poor figure in a Dickens' novel,

identifying with the downtrodden to whom good fortune unexpectedly arrives. One of her great-aunts even compared her arrival in
the Commerce Street house as being like the arrival of a foundling,
"like someone just left a baby out on our doorstep." ("Sleepytown,
1992")

But Tartt also found Dickens a "benevolent presence" for the
aspiring young writer. Dickens was an important presence in her
memories of early childhood, too. She's said that books spoke to
her childhood self with an English accent, and she appears to
Anglicize her own ancestry: her great-grandfather wasn't just born
in the nineteenth century (1887): she thought of him (non-
problematically) as a Victorian. Perhaps more problematically, he
seemed to think of her as a Victorian, too. He remained convinced
that his great granddaughter, like his own younger sister, would die
in early childhood and would prophesy her demise during some of
her more feverish nights.

From around the age of ten, she was beginning to derive from
her great-grandfather an awareness of the importance of writers who
were "great prose stylist[s]." Favored recipients of this accolade were
Thomas de Quincey and James Fenimore Cooper (Bunny's taunting "Deerslayer" references after the bacchanal also chime with
Fenimore Cooper's novel of that name, posing a stark contrast
between the honorable, truthful and pure hero of Cooper's work
and Tartt's corrupt, misguided protagonists). Dickens, however,
tended to be singled out in particular, as though he were also a
personal friend. These early lessons were ones she learned well: "I
know at heart I'm-I'm-I'm a manic stylist" she told one London
interviewer.[5]

Other early (and related) interests were in all things gothic and
in Victorian murders. She kept an old cigar box underneath her
bed full of things that she treasured. But hidden underneath all the
bric-a-bric was a secret photographic slide, stolen from her uncle,

depicting "savages, on some horrid African veld, eating a bloody and dismembered thing", a thing she was sure was a person. Afraid to touch it, but fortified by her medicine, she would look at it, aware of a discordance she would write about years later in her own work. As a child, she was both riveted by the obvious horror of the scene, even as she observed (or believed) that it had no power to affect her (though she dreamed of observing demonic rituals involving the barbecuing of live Persian cats). The metamorphosis from the photograph's capture of bloody event to becoming the subject of abstract speculation is re-articulated in one of Julian Morrow's seminars: "But how is it that such a ghastly thing, a queen stabbing her husband in his bath, is so lovely to us?" asks Julian. (*The Secret History*, p. 37) The answer lies in Aristotle's *Poetics*, ventures Henry, that what is painful to view in itself can be transfigured in a work of art. "And I believe Aristotle is correct" Julian goes on, unwittingly endorsing their planned bacchanal. It is with distaste that some of the reviewers of *The Secret History* noted that the farmer's disemboweled body seems hardly to signify in the narrative after the event. But the process of transfiguration is arguably at work: it's not the brutal murder that concerns anyone (except for the non-classical Bunny) but rather our own (and Richard's) attempt to understand what prompts the desire to return to the ancient ritual.

She has also recalled loving "beyond reason" a collection of stories that she shared with her mother about Victorian murders, called *Blood in the Parlour*.[6] What she liked about the murder cases was the discrepancy between appearance and reality: it was just this discrepancy that would come to underline *The Secret History*. And discrepant is how Tartt emerges in all her different profiles. She looked different, and she behaved different.

In 1981, she attended the University of Mississippi, Oxford (Ole Miss). She pledged herself to a sorority, but cut an incongruous and eccentric figure. She was distinctive anyway, small and dark-haired amidst a group of towering blondes. But in her *Vanity Fair* interview with James Kaplan, she admitted to him what she would not admit to her "Kappa Kappa Gamma" sorority: that she had placed ominous messages in the Sunshine Box saying "God is dead . . . And we have killed him." She read Ezra Pound's *Cantos* in the rain and sat alone in the Union reading Nietzsche and claimed to be "so happy. Not lonely." She struck Willie Morris, then the writer-in-residence at Ole Miss, as grown-up but also childlike (like her mother, who could be both graceful and "Baby"). And he also sensed that she had, somewhere in the past, Suffered.

The Tartt legend really began after she unsuccessfully submitted articles to the college paper. She was approached by Morris who said: "My name is Willie Morris and I think you're a genius." On his advice, Tartt left the University of Mississippi and transferred to Bennington, the liberal arts college in Vermont (on which *The Secret History*'s Hampden College is rumored to be based, a rumor she denies, although Bennington as a location does feature on occasion in the novel, p. 430). A mannered, stylized and stylish figure emerges from the recollections of her Bennington contemporaries who have described her as controlled and "very put-together" (*Vanity Fair*, 1992) as though at Bennington she remade herself, a notion underlined by Kaplan's observation that "she is, somehow, a character of her own fictive creation." (*Vanity Fair*, 1992). Green-eyed, tiny (as a baby she wore doll's clothes), well-tailored, insomniac (like Richard, p. 68 and Henry, p. 79), chain-smoking and heavy drinking (Ellis claimed that she could drink him under the table and still retain a composed dignity) she remained an eccentric figure, once reading P. G. Wodehouse aloud to calm a group of truly confused friends who had "been up all night for days." (sic) (*Vanity Fair*, 1992) (P. G. Wodehouse is what

Richard takes to the distressed Charles to cheer him up in hospital, a gesture which fails to comprehend the seriousness of his physical illness and depression.)

And the rest is a not so secret history. She found creative writing classes at Bennington both bemusing and stifling, and claimed never to have heard of minimalism when "Back then it was all minimalism, minimalism, minimalism . . .".[7] She resisted attempts to turn her into a sub-Raymond Carver, and became part of a select and well-dressed clique of self-contained students clustered around one tutor, Claude Fredericks, described as "a brilliant but odd teacher who admitted few people to his classes" and who taught Greek (*Vanity Fair*, 1992); Tartt was the only woman in the group. She is also said to have developed a close friendship with Paul McGloin (her novel was dedicated to him and Bret (Easton Ellis)) the description of whom (physically, sartorially and intellectually) bears more than a passing resemblance to Henry Winter (at least, how he appears to Richard in Book I). It was during her second year at Bennington that she began to write *The Secret History*:

My first novel came to me quite unexpectedly, but very persistently for all that, during six months that I had taken off from college to study Latin. At the end of that time, I had made it only partway through the Latin text I was supposed to have finished, but I had quite a little stack of work of my own which ended up, six or seven years later, becoming a book.[8]

She showed the manuscript-in-progress to fellow student Bret Easton Ellis. He expressed one reservation, that Richard was a sexless figure. Tartt's responding glare froze him, but his comment clearly troubled her, since she has located sex as important to the novel's hinterland. Otherwise, Ellis assured her that the novel had the makings of a commercial success, which surprised her since she felt that its length and erudition ("The book's got Greek phrases")[9] would surely preclude it from the bestseller ranks.

But she was wrong, and Ellis was right. Since the publication of *The Secret History*, Tartt has published little: some short fiction, book reviews, essays. Her long-awaited second novel is still — well, long awaited. Any consideration of quite where *The Secret History* fits in her *oeuvre* is considerably curtailed by the fact that, to date, *The Secret History* substantially constitutes her *oeuvre*. To some extent, the extant body of her work suggests an interest in aspects of illusion and reality, fact and fiction and an interest in the figure of the outsider. (See section 5.)

Speculation about her second novel abounds. In 1993 Tartt said she was reading Thomas Burton's *Serpent Handling Believers* as research for her second novel. In another immediately post-publication interview for *The Secret History* she promised that the second book was going to be more ambiguous and elliptical than the first: "it's really about how do we know what's true and what's false." (*Newsday*, April 10, 1992). While this ambiguity chimes well with *The Secret History*, and indeed with the fantastic and social speculations and implications of her shorter fiction and "True Crime", it's also proved prophetic in terms of precisely when and where this novel is going to appear. In 1997, one source told a journalist that the book was about a sister's investigation into her brother's suicide. A Random House web-site indicated that the new book was called *Henry Darger*, explaining that "The author of *The Secret History* explores the creative and the business sides of modern art, focusing on the work of Henry Darger, a primitive artist and an art-world outsider whose work was discovered only after his death — work that is provocative, beautiful, controversial and quite disturbing." Brett Easton Ellis is reported to have said that Tartt had lost the manuscript she was working on, went through a period of mourning, and then began again. In her "Talk of the Nation" interview with Ray Suarez, Tartt assured listeners that the book would be out very soon. Random House claimed that the book was due out for Christmas 1998. And then the book was said to be coming out in Spring 2000, and again, in September 2001, called *Tribulation*. According to a BBC Radio interview broadcast on June 19th 2001, the novel is still entitled *Tribulation*. Tartt said, "It's a book about children, but not for children. It's a frightening, scary book about children coming into contact with the world of adults in a very frightening way." At the time of writing, the book is scheduled for publication in February 2002.

Contrary to the evidence of this erudite and literate book, Tartt has said that what inspires her to write is not the intellect but something more mystical, inspired by her *daimon* or "divine spirit." Indeed, Tartt's religious beliefs (expressed in a recent essay[10]) have prompted her to see the novel as having a divine or spiritual function:

A good novel . . . enables non-believers to participate in a world-view that religious people take for granted: life as a vast polyphonous web of interconnections, predestined meetings, fortuitous choices and accidents, all governed by a unifying if unforseen plan. Insofar as novels shed light on human existence, this is how they do it."[11]

The Secret History does indeed offer these interconnections, fortuitous choices and accidents. Quite what light Tartt's novel sheds on human existence is one of the issues that the next section will address.

POSSIBLE INFLUENCES

When the reviews of *The Secret History* came out, many compared Tartt's novel (usually to disparage it) with those of her Bennington contemporary, Bret Easton Ellis. Comparisons are actually quite limiting. Ellis's narrative style is very different to Tartt's. His some-times fractured narrative mode mimics the often rabid lifestyles that his protagonists endure rather than enjoy. Thus, they can begin or end mid-sentence, as though they can't be bothered to introduce or complete themselves, and new, sometimes desperate, isolated nar-rative voices appear then just as quickly disappear from view. *Less Than Zero*, written while he was still at Bennington, in some ways offers a lament for a lost innocence as Clay witnesses the moral degradation and sexual exploitation of his friends while he's at home during the Christmas vacation. That they are all privileged, unloved and utterly self-centered offers some comparison to aspects of *The Secret History*, as well as to his second novel, *The Rules of Attrac-tion*. Explicit reference is made on two occasions in that novel to what was then the embryonic *The Secret History*:

But who *doesn't* go to The Dressed to Get Screwed Party, besides that weird Classics group (and they're probably roaming the countryside sacrific-ing farmers and performing pagan rituals)? (Stuart, p. 179)

That weird group of Classics majors stand by, looking like undertakers. (Lauren, p. 259)

While his first novel focused on the vacation, his second is firmly placed on the campus of 'Camden' college, and the casual and frequent sexual exploits of its denizens. One character, Sean Bate-man, has a brother, Patrick, who then comes into his infamous and horrible own in Ellis's third novel, *American Psycho*, appearing just a year before *The Secret History*. One small possible allusion to *The Secret History* is evident in a discussion about 'Camden': "Oh great," I say, "Some chick who thinks it's okay to fuck her brother." (33) Though Patrick Bateman announces that "Our lives are *not* all interconnected" (217) one can see a progression of sorts through

Ellis's first three novels, with Bateman as a not unexpected spawn of late twentieth century post-modern America, as well as offering a scathing satire on its corrupt values. ". . . there is an idea of a Patrick Bateman, some kind of abstraction, but there is no real me, only an entity, something illusory . . ." he tells his innocent secretary Jean. Patrick's inability to feel, together with his sense that he doesn't exist are crises of identity also explored in *The Secret History*. One last nod in the direction of *The Secret History* may well be at the moment Patrick patiently explains to Jean, as they sit in a restaurant called "Arcadia," that its namesake was destroyed: its nominal incarnation in the contemporary nightmare of America exists, perhaps, to mock the damned who may well mourn a paradise lost.

Readers may recognise a homage of sorts to Dostoevsky's *Crime and Punishment* (1865–1866) which explores the psychology of guilt after a violent crime. Notably, the student murderer Raskolnikov decides that Lizaveta, the pawnbroker he murdered, was unloved and old so that her death somehow matters less.

Richard's journey, in taking him from the moribund culture of the American West (California) to the apparent promise of Arcadia in the East (Hampden), recalls *The Great Gatsby*'s (1926) narrator Nick Carraway, who also takes in that East Coast decadence and excessive material wealth which seems as symptomatic of an enervated America in the early twentieth century as it does at the century's end. In Richard's case, the journey from West to East involves the self-defeating attempt to resuscitate one dead culture (vapid and consumerist America) with another (that of classical antiquity). But the social issues of old versus new (or no) money is as much at the heart of *The Secret History* as it is at the heart of *The Great Gatsby*, and the novels seem at times to be like equivalents of the "twin town." At one point, Bunny resembles Tom Buchanan: his inquisition about Richard's school (TSH, pp. 208–210) echoes Tom's interrogation about Gatsby's alleged time at the University of

Oxford. The auto repair man Bill Hundy is obviously no Tom Buchanan, but like Tom, he consistently speaks for a white America. And Richard (pompously? pretentiously?) identifies with the doomed and self-made Jay Gatsby; he does not know himself well enough to see that he is closer to *The Great Gatsby*'s narrator, Nick Carraway, making his journey from innocence to experience.

Innocence and experience are mapped through Richard's belief that he has found his Arcadia, followed by his recognition that his belief was illusionary. Although Evelyn Waugh's *Brideshead Revisited* (1945) is not alluded to directly (as *Crime and Punishment* and *The Great Gatsby* are), the main similarities occur in Book 1, "Et in Arcadia Ego" (and even in Arcadia I), which might well have served as an epigraph for Book I of *The Secret History*. Any comparison with *Brideshead Revisited* establishes themes of innocence or paradise lost during the "languor of Youth" as Waugh describes it. Add a dreamy university location, infatuation with a glamorous group of undergraduates, a country house which offers a retreat from the outside world in which friendships are cemented and unmade, a brother and sister who closely resemble each other and provide a sexual *frisson*, and you can see why reviewers made the connections. Both books explore (amongst other things) the exoticism and banality of decadence in their respective epochs. And although Tartt does give Richard time to frolic in the bucolic at Francis's country house, it isn't long before "all Cyrene bowed her head, to see the home of happy children made desolate" (TSH, p. 190) and, one way or another, he realizes that in truth, they are all damned by their actions, and there will be no redemption.

Readers may also wish to read John Fowles's *The Magus* (1966). In his foreword to the Revised Edition (1976) he commented on the importance of Jung and Alain-Fournier's *Le Grand Meaulnes* as influences on his text, singling out *Le Grand Meaulnes* in particular for its "capacity . . . to provide an experience beyond the literary"

(p. 6). Fowles also claimed that he came to realize that Dickens's *Great Expectations* was also an unconscious influence on *The Magus*. Nicholas, a young Englishman, takes a job teaching English in a boys school on a Greek island. He's soon inveigled into the mysterious world of the wealthy and well-connected Conchis, whose life is the stuff of myth and lies. Nicholas begins to spend his weekends at Bourani, Conchis's house, in which he learns that truth and fiction are repeatedly interchangeable; he is wrong-footed so often that he no longer knows what, or who, to believe. Conchis has a mysterious past, the truth of which is repeatedly confirmed and then exposed as a fiction, and Nicholas is drawn both willingly and unwillingly into a world of illusion and theatre and hallucination where acting and authenticity are confused so many times that they no longer have any meaning. Although Conchis says that he longs for the return of Apollo, and wishes to banish Dionysus to the shadows (p. 186), he keeps a tight control over a very ordered chaos. He orchestrates a world where the dead appear to live, where recent history (the Nazi occupation of the Greek islands) is repeated, and where figures from Greek mythology ("I was the Eumenides, the merciless Furies", p. 515) appear to have a real existence. Conchis's manipulation and control of his young actors and actresses, though infinitely more sinister and pronounced than Julian's nurturing of his own students, is still worth comparing.

2

The Novel[1]

INTRODUCTION

The Plot

The Secret History is a confessional novel, and rather like Coleridge's Ancient Mariner, Richard Papen, the book's narrator, is fated to have only one story to tell. His retrospective narrative is told as atonement for his complicity in the murder of his classmate, Bunny Corcoran, one of a small and élite group of friends studying Classics at Hampden College, Vermont. Book I engages with Richard's journey from West Coast California to Hampden College in East Coast Vermont. Once there, he finds himself smitten with a group of five distinctive Classics students, Henry Winter, Edmund "Bunny" Corcoran, Francis Abernathy, and the twins, Charles and Camilla Macaulay. After a chance meeting, he manages to inveigle his way into their extremely selective classes, taught by the apparently mysterious and enchanting figure of Julian Morrow. One seminar in particular, on telesic or ritual madness (whose god is Dionysus), inspires the group, led by Henry, to perform a bacchanal in which they can relinquish their civilized, conscious selves to a liberated, primitive abandon. They decide to exclude Bunny, who can't take their preparations for the bacchanal seriously, thus putting into jeopardy their careful plans. But the best laid plans cannot cover all eventualities, and the group, while out of their minds, mutilate a local Vermont farmer who finds them at the height of their wild frenzy on his land. Bunny, finding the newspaper coverage of this, begins to suspect what they have done, and hectors them about it. His behavior becomes increasingly boorish, principally because he'd been left out of the bacchanal. And then he discovers (by reading Henry's diary) that they did indeed kill the farmer. Thereafter, he blackmails and insults and threatens the group who, led by Henry, murder him to save themselves from being caught by pushing him over a ravine.

Though this is meant to look like a simple hiking accident, an unexpected and deep snowfall covers the body for days, and an enormous manhunt is launched for Bunny, involving local and federal police. Tartt then anatomizes their guilt and remorse, stepping up the suspense by dropping in several red herrings as the detectives follow one bizarre lead after another and the fate of Bunny's corpse acquires, so to speak, a life of its own. Once the snow melts Bunny's body is quickly discovered, and the group, now suffering individually and to very different degrees, begin to slowly break down as the enormity of what they've done comes home to them. A chance discovery of a letter in which Bunny confides to Julian that he thinks Henry is going to kill him leads Julian to abandon the group he has created and nurtured, although he will not betray them to the police. Henry, deeply wounded by this rejection, subsequently kills himself, Charles becomes alcoholic, Francis attempts suicide and Camilla and Richard are doomed to lead unhappy, unfulfilled lives. Richard in particular feels great compunction for his involvement in Bunny's death, especially after his realization that they had all acted under Henry's strong manipulative and sinister control.

MAJOR THEMES

Divided into two books, the novel is sandwiched between an enticing Prologue and an ultimately mystifying Epilogue. At the end of his story, some ten years after the events he narrates, Richard tells us that in order to make sense of this brief period of his life, he has become a literary scholar, studying Jacobean Tragedy, (drama pertaining to the reign of James I (1603–25)). He finds Jacobean drama appealing for "the candlelit and treacherous universe in which they moved—of sin unpunished, of innocence destroyed . . . Even the titles of their plays were strangely seductive, trapdoors to something beautiful and wicked that trickled beneath the surface of mortality." (TSH, p. 512) This, then, is what he perceives his narrative to be about: sin unpunished, innocence destroyed, and secret, subterranean impulses masked by something more ordinary. There's much in these comments that open up *The Secret History* to a reading that speaks to more than the themes of innocence and sin or appearance and reality. For one thing, it's spectacle and theatre, acting and dissembling, that offers him an understanding of his own experiences. These issues are integral to the book, speaking not only to the official or secret history which sustains the story, but also to the search for an authentic self and an alternative culture which proves, in the end, to be the classicists' undoing. And in coming to understand his actions through the sensibilities and conventions of a specific literary genre, Richard intimates either that life follows art, or that life is only rendered meaningful or sensible within a literary—and literate—culture. Books, that is to say, make sense of books, a notion that will be developed later in this section.

GENRE

Such a summary plot reading raises questions (if not eyebrows). For *The Secret History* shifts register several times between a world that is recognizable and rational, and between one that seems surreal and unknowable, between our culture and an ancient one. For some readers, this may stretch the credibility of the realist narrative but in suspending realism, the narrative opens up a different space of unbounded imaginative play. The novel requires of us, then, the kind of faith that Henry realizes he must have if his bacchanal is to work. In fact, if we were to sub-divide the book, it begins as a murder story, albeit with a difference, since who copped it and whodunnit are revealed in the first paragraphs. The only element of suspense left to us is *why*, although actually, this doesn't take long to discover.

Richard gives us the illusion from the beginning that he has a real or "extra-textual" status outside the pages of the text: does the fatal flaw exist outside literature, he asks, and answers his own question, yes it does, putting his own whereabouts outside the fictive frame. He presents himself as an ordinary, unremarkable young man who leaves his equally ordinary and unremarkable home town to go to college. The narrative then warms to its themes: Richard's bedazzlement with his surroundings and new friends makes possible his unwitting seduction into evil. The intellectual inspiration for the bacchanal is outlined, providing some explanation and understanding for it. Richard's contentment increases at Francis's country house, where four of the friends begin to exhibit strange behavioral patterns which will also later explain the bacchanal. And one fault line runs throughout: Bunny Corcoran's muted tendencies to be a vulgar, racist, xenophobic and homophobic bully gradually crescendo, rendering him a loudly obnoxious figure. Our sympathy works *if* we've identified with Richard, since we see it all (with one or two exceptions) through his narrative perspective. Realism transmutes into a kind of magic realism, in which reality and illusion obtrude upon each other in the Dionysian ritual which is replete with orgies, visions and hallucinations, but which ends with such horrifying consequences. Following the apparent disappearance of Bunny, the detective elements of the book then dominate. The dissection of guilt and the realization that Henry is a sinister manipulator conclude proceedings. In short, the novel is realist and it's surrealist. It functions partly as detective/murder mystery fiction as it anatomizes the story of a crime. It draws attention to its status as literature with continuous references to other literary texts, inviting comparisons and distinctions, and providing a measure for how we may come to assess the book. But all of these generic elements tend to be interdependent, and Tartt's themes evolve and develop through them. In order to further explicate these, this section will expand on some of the main issues in the novel. Because these are interdependent, there will be a certain amount of overlap and return, but otherwise, the section follows the chronology of the events in the text.

CHANCE AND FATE

Richard suggests that his arrival at Hampden was destined: "I lit on Hampden by a trick of fate" (TSH, p. 11) as he recalls his opportune discovery of the college prospectus. Chance or fate then determines events, from his first encounter with Bunny, Charles and Camilla in the library, to Bunny's inordinately *in*opportune meeting with Henry *et al* at the edge of the ravine. If we are to read these events as being somehow predetermined, as if they had already been written or scripted, then two small but related questions emerge: why, and to what end? Richard's sense of Fate suggests that his story has already been written, but since *The Secret History* is such a bookish book, in a sense, he's right: it has. *The Secret History* is so strewn with allusions to the Western literary and classical canon that the extent of the borrowing is difficult to ignore. Although the last part of this section addresses some of these borrowings, a great many of the allusions support, if they do not actually constitute, one of the important themes of the novel: the relationship of the mediocre present to the heroic past, a relationship which seduces the classicists into rejecting their own atrophied culture and abandoning what it is to *be* in the modern world in favor of a single, isolated aspect of Greek thought. Since they have all been acculturated in the modern world, (in spite of Henry's ignorance of twentieth century iconography) they also replicate its structures and behaviors. The violence and racism described in pockets of the local Vermont society are evidence of an "in" group turning on an "out group." And Richard's narrative traces the consequences of what happens when the inner sanctum (Henry, Francis, Charles and Camilla) invite one outsider (Richard) in, to help emphasize quite how "outside" Bunny has become. Henry's desire to return to the mindset of an older culture means that rather than escaping a culture he despises, he ends up replicating some of its most invidious characteristics.

BEGINNINGS

Hampden is presented in stark contrast to the unlovely environment of Plano, and like one of Richard's first encounters with Francis, it is at once material and apparently phantasmal. Hailing from the cultural and visual meagerness of Plano where nothing predates 1962, he gorges himself on Hampden: "Trees creaking with apples, fallen apples red on the grass beneath, the heavy sweet smell of them rotting on the ground and the steady thrumming of wasps around them." (TSH, p. 13) Blinded by his new prejudices, he cannot recognize the remnants of his old ones. Of Plano, he had complained in his journal: "There is to me about this place a smell of rot, the smell of rot that ripe fruit makes." (TSH, p. 10) Only later, after the murder, can he re-evaluate his life in Plano not as a companion piece to *Paradise Lost* (as he imagines it) or as a place of decay, but as a place of decency and innocence. At Hampden, Richard decides to reinvent his drab and secret history, "disposable as a plastic cup" (TSH, p. 8). His father (like Bill Hundy) runs a gas station, his mother answers phones, but he transforms his familiar and hated world of shopping malls and muzak into a different American dream of orange groves and swimming pools complete with "charming show-biz parents." (As the narrator who shapes the story, he has much in common with the author who animates the narrator: "Basically, we all lie for a living . . ." Tartt has said[2].) Notably, the only person who he believes is impressed (and who he assumes believes him, though we can never know for sure) is Julian: "Never had my efforts met with such attentiveness, such keen solic-itude" (TSH 26–7). Julian (who, shrouded as he is in mystery, is something of a Gatsby figure himself) intrigues Richard, though since he doesn't even try to convey Julian's apparent brilliance, the nature of it often seems puzzling in the novel, and their devotion (Richard's at any rate) is prompted more by his own emotional impoverishment than by anything more compelling in Julian: ". . . it was Julian who had grown to be the sole figure of paternal benevolence in my life . . . To me, he seemed my only protector in the world." (TSH, p. 475)

SETTING THE SCENE: AT THE LYCEUM

When Richard does finally speak to Julian's chosen group, huddled together in the library and puzzling over what is in fact a fairly basic Greek composition, it seems as if "the characters in a favourite painting, absorbed in their own concerns, had looked up out of the canvas and spoken to me." (TSH, p. 21) His next encounter with them should be enough to dispel his illusions, but it isn't: the evanescent Francis makes a sexual proposition — *Cubitum eamus?* — which Richard either doesn't understand, or affects not to hear. In Julian's Lyceum, Bunny is squabbling with Henry who's just bought a Mont Blanc fountain pen: "You," said Henry sharply, "are not one to speak of taste." (TSH, p. 32) Bunny's sly barbs are evident even from this early encounter — "And you, what's-your-name, Robert? What sort of pens did they teach you to use in California?" (TSH, p. 33) (Though he uses ball-points, prompting Bunny to declare him an honest man, he gives them up for the fountain pens the others use. After the murder, Charles offers to copy Richard's Greek for him with his fountain pen (TSH, p. 279) implying that if a man's pen, as Bunny infers, is a sign of his integrity, then Richard's days of honesty are over.) In this first meeting, too, Henry is critical of Richard, exposing his ignorance, and reminding him of a policeman asking questions (a sign of things to come?). Indeed, as he begins to animate them they *appear* to be a squabbling, unfriendly and arrogant group. So why does he like them?

Several reasons suggest themselves. On the one hand, this may be a strategic device, to reveal the extent of Richard's infatuation with them: he puts them on a pedestal, we see them as distinctly more prosaic figures. On the other hand, since Richard offers no real comment on their behavior (other than to reveal his own discomfort with Henry's line of questioning) the scene may also allows us a space to see them as fairly ordinary individuals: Henry is competitive, Bunny is teasing, deflating Henry's pretensions, Francis has a tendency towards camp, Charles and Camilla (the most ill-defined character in the book) are considerate and sweet. And so they might have continued, except that their actions pervert what might be seen as benign characteristics. Competitiveness becomes manipulative control, teasing about expensive pens becomes extortion, camp becomes peevishness, and the twins Richard remembers as kind and sweet become, in the case of Charles, violent and resentful and, in the case of Camilla, passive and acquiescent. Reviewers tended to criticize Tartt's characterization of the group as cardboard figures, and certainly Camilla seems to fare worst of all since she appears through the soft-focus lens of Richard's desire, framed in one light or another, honey-hued as Humbert Humbert's Lolita. Or she is passively acquiescent in the relationship with Charles (she offers no resistance when he kisses her in front of Richard) and finally in her relationship with Henry, when he appears at his most strange and mechanical. The group are also conveyed through set characteristics or appearance: Camilla tends to be framed in light, Henry's spectacles always seem to be glinting, Bunny seems to be slack-jawed, his trousers knee-sprung, his hands always thrust deep into the pockets of his jacket, hair flopping, while the red-haired Francis stalks campus like a theatrical figure sporting props, the plain glass pince-nez, his black coat flapping behind him. Charles's appearance is the least defined, best visualized, perhaps, during his decline. The appeal for Richard, in the beginning at least, is their wealth and appearance. He enjoys being in the restaurant with Bunny: "I was well aware of the impression we were making—two handsome college boys, rich fathers and not a worry in the world." (TSH, p. 47) Yet if the reviewers were critical of characterization, the popularity of the book suggests that whether the characters are attractive or repulsive, they're compelling as individuals and in terms of the different dynamics that operate within their group. Youth, wealth, looks, leisure are, after all, highly prized in contemporary (not to mention Graeco-Roman) culture.

JUDY POOVEY

Most prominent amongst the other campus figures is the fast-talking, essentially kind-hearted Judy Poovey. As she is the main representative of the dominant social type of student at Hampden, we can also read her at a functional level, and see her as another narrative device who circumvents the limitations of Richard's single perspective and biased descriptions of the classicists. It's Judy who first suggests that there's something menacing about them, and more importantly, indicates Henry's strength and imposing physical presence. For although she considers him a "sissy" (for wearing a suit) she also speak of him with some awe for the night he broke the collar bone of Spike Romney, one of the toughest students on campus. But though Judy sounds a warning, like the Good Angel in a morality play, Richard is still too besotted with Henry to think about his capacity for violence. Instead, his infatuation with them all results in his selection of vignettes which is intended to show them off at their languorous and youthful best, before their subsequent actions come to delimit them, leaving them old beyond their years.

'ET IN ARCADIA EGO'

His continued defense of the group to the other students at Campden suggests that the cumulative drip, drip, drip of his entrancement is at work all the time. And he surely sounds the knell of all their dooms when he refers to feeling as though he's on the *Titanic* when first at Francis's country house. His weekends at Francis's aunt's house seem filtered through an older literary sensibility, particularly the first book of Evelyn Waugh's *Brideshead Revisited*, "Et in Arcadia Ego" where Charles Ryder and Sebastian Flyte cement their friendship at Brideshead, Sebastian's aristocratic country home and where they spend an idyllic summer isolated and apart from the criticisms that bedevil them at Oxford and elsewhere. The collections of Francis's bibliophile aunt seem representative of a retreat from the campus life of Judy and the other students, but also more generally, from late twentieth century America. The books that she has collected, from the *Bobbsey Twins* to Thomas Pennant's *London* to an 1821 first edition of Byron's *Marino Falerio*, suggest a retreat to a world of eighteenth and nineteenth century England and Europe, and a more innocent American childhood. Only Bunny brings trappings of the twentieth century: Sax Rohmer's *The Bride of Fu Manchu* in which the zvengali Dr. Fu Manchu exercises manipulative and evil control over an innocent young woman (all in pursuit of world domination, naturally). So seductive is the world that they have created there that Charles and Richard imagine living in it forever (a domestic and anchored version of their toast, to live forever). This idyll will involve Bunny returning at weekends (leaving Marion and their children at home). Actually, this looks like another harbinger of death; when Bunny talks about having children, Henry tells him "about how the fulfilment of the reproductive cycle was, in nature, an invariable harbinger of swift decline and death." (TSH, p. 96) And it's here, too, that a desperate Charles wants to return and hide with Richard following his last great argument with Henry as the novel stalks towards its terrible conclusions. (TSH, p. 419) But although this environment seems appropriate for characters who, incredibly, don't know that men had walked on the moon or haven't heard of Marilyn Monroe, there are still signs of doom aplenty, even in their self-made Arcadia. Thus, Richard's borrowed (and consequently inauthentic) memories involve "Parties on sinking ships . . ." (TSH, p. 7) and Francis sings "We are little black sheep who have gone astray . . ." (TSH, p. 96) and "Gentlemen songsters *off* on a spree . . . Doomed from here to *eternity* . . ." (TSH, p. 97) These are juxtaposed with Richard's desire to live there forever in what he fixes as his paradise lost:

The idea of living there, of not having to go back ever again to asphalt and shopping malls and modular furniture; of living there with Charles and Camilla and Henry and Francis and maybe even Bunny; of no one marrying or going home or getting a job in a town a thousand miles away or doing any of the traitorous things friends do after college; of everything remaining exactly as it was, that instant—the idea was so truly heavenly that I'm not sure I thought, even then, it could ever really happen, but I like to believe I did." (TSH, p. 97)

As his delight intensifies each distilled recollection reveals his childlike delight, from Bunny's excitement at the first snow of the year (irony surely intended?) to Camilla's teaching him how to box step. Yet all the while, he remains outside the intellectual and spiritual dynamic of the core members of the group, now reduced to four, and preparing for their bacchanal.

ECHOES OF DANTE

When Bunny first suggests it's a pity that Richard isn't in their class, he recalls Charles and Camilla's ensuing and strained silence. Why he's accepted into this close knit group who have shared classes together for at least two years is never really made clear. After all, when he first encounters them in the library, it was Camilla who was right, not Richard: "If the Greeks are sailing *to* Carthage, it should be accusative." (TSH, p. 19) Strategically, we could argue that Tartt required an outsider with some emotional distance from them to enter the group and then report on the events. And since Richard can't recall the substance of the interview with Julian (beyond his own lies about his show business family, orange groves and swimming pools), we never see how he convincingly wins Julian over to accept him in his class. (Unless, of course, it's Julian's penchant for glamorous film stars that does the trick.) But if the narrative itself can't offer a convincing answer beyond the requirements of plot, then perhaps another avenue of exploration might be worth thinking about. For although the group's acceptance of Richard into their fold is initially grudging, it is nonetheless an acceptance, and it carries intimations of another text which is explicitly referred to several times in the narrative.

In *Inferno*, the first book of *The Divine Comedy*, Dante is beckoned to join the poets of Greek antiquity as he descends into the first circle of Hell. Dante, with Virgil as his guide, is joined by Homer, Horace, Ovid, and Lucan:

> *And greater honour yet they did me—yea,*
> *Into their fellowship they deigned invite*
> *And make me sixth among such minds as they.*
>
> *So we moved slowly on toward the light*
> *In talk 'twere as unfitting to repeat*
> *Here, as to speak there was both fit and right.*
> (Canto IV, l.100–105)

Aspects of Hampden life remind Richard specifically of Dante: he regards the writhing bodies at one of the parties he goes to as "a Dantesque mass of bodies on the dance floor." (TSH, p. 69) Charles dreams that Dante is with him at the Corcoran house (TSH, p. 445), Bunny takes *Inferno* (the Dorothy Sayers translation, cited here) to Italy, and Henry wields a copy of *Purgatorio* whilst he's planning to murder Bunny. Just as Richard now makes up the sixth member of the group, so Tartt intimates a more sinister fate is beckoning, and the anticipation of their damnation begins, as though it has already been scripted, from Canto I:

> *Midway this way of life we're bound upon,*
> *I woke to find myself in a dark wood,*
> *Where the right road was wholly lost and gone.*
> (Canto I, l.1–3)

to Canto XII, in which Virgil and Dante face a ravine strewn with rocks, which will take them into the Seventh Circle of Hell.

REHEARSING THE BACCHANAL

Rather like a dumb-show, the theatrical device that silently acts out the main events of a play before they are fully performed, the early action of *The Secret History* begins to unfold in Richard's first seminar. Julian introduces the thesis: the burden of being, the isolation of the self as an integral condition of being, the torment of our inner demons from which we would like to escape, and the desire to transcend the affliction of selfhood (all of which Richard is fated to experience keenly). They discuss Plato's four divine madnesses, (though not named in the text, they are Apollo's prophetic madness, Dionysus's telestic or ritual madness, poetic madness inspired by the Muses, and the erotic madness of Eros and Aphrodite). Of the four, it is really telestic or ritual madness that occupies them that afternoon. Referring to "that obstinate little voice" that torments us, Julian invites them to meditate upon their own mortality as well as to recognize that we are truly alone in our suffering. To compound our sense of isolation, we must also come to realize as we grow older that we never truly understand one another, no matter how deep our love for one another might be. Even the doltish, gum-chewing Bunny is "dazzled" by Julian's speech about the Furies who "turned up the volume of the inner monologue, magnified qualities already present to great excess, made people so much *themselves* that they couldn't stand it." (TSH, p. 35) Significantly, what is absent from Julian's description is the notion of punishment, since the Furies (conceived from the spilled blood of a crime committed by son against father) avenge wrongs, especially murder within the family. (In the end, Henry's wrongs *are* avenged when he receives the greatest punishment possible: Julian both abandons and, as Henry sees it, betrays him: "I loved him more than my own father," he said. "I loved him more than anyone in the world." TSH, p. 487)

After the prologue-thesis comes a rehearsal of what the group will go on to enact in their bacchanal. Julian points out to them the discrepancy between violence as an experience and violence transformed in art, which can be beautiful to behold. To illustrate, Julian asks Camilla to recite what she remembers from Klytemnestra's speech in the *Oresteia*:

> *Thus he died, and all the life struggled out of him;*
> *and as he died he spattered me with the dark red*
> *and violent-driven rain of bitter-savored blood*
> *to make me glad, as gardens stand among the showers*
> *of God in glory at the birthtime of the buds.*
>
> (TSH, p. 36)

Charles and Francis proffer their interpretations as to why the passage should seem so beautiful even though it is so violent. For them, form is more significant than content, and the meter or rhythm of the piece is what constitutes its aesthetic value. But Henry offers the interpretation that Julian endorses: what is most painful to behold can be wonderful to think about in its artistic representation, so that beauty and terror are implicated, one in the other. Julian then leads them on to think about the nature of desire. Bunny (ironically) knows what we most desire: it is to live forever. This becomes talismanic for the bacchantes (i.e., Henry, Francis, Charles, Camilla) as well as for the entire group, terrible and tragic on the one hand, alluring and innocent on the other. Richard remembers it as part of the idyllic and dreamlike world of Francis's country house:

There is a recurrent scene from those dinners that surfaces again and again, like an obsessive undercurrent in a dream. Julian at the head of the long table rises to his feet and lifts his wineglass. "Live forever," he says.

And the rest of us rise too, and clink our glasses across the table, like an army regiment crossing sabres: Henry and Bunny, Charles and Francis, Camilla and I. "Live forever," we chorus, throwing our glasses back in unison.

And always, always, that same toast. Live forever. (TSH, p. 86)

THE DIONYSIAN

Henry wants to achieve what Julian describes: "The revelers were apparently hurled back into a non-rational, pre-intellectual state, where the personality was replaced by something completely different—and by 'different' I mean something to all appearances not mortal. Inhuman." (TSH, p. 38) And he goes on to repeat a notion familiarized by Freud in "Civilization and Its Discontents": that civilization is built on the repression of primal, instinctive and sexual urges. But Julian goes further: it is a mistake to try and repress or "murder" the primitive self. Richard is uncomfortable with all this, but Julian's apostles are captivated as he finishes with his final persuasive push, that it is more than a mistake, it is "dangerous" to ignore the irrational: the greater the repression, the more savage the backlash (Bret Easton Ellis's Patrick Bateman comes to mind here, the epitome of the cultivated, if uptight, professional and discerning consumer in public; monstrously and sadistically pornographic and murderous in private). For Henry, who worships Julian as a divinity, this final flourish sounds the death knell:

"If we are strong enough in our souls we can rip away the veil and look that naked, terrible beauty right in the face; let God consume us, devour us, unstring our bones. Then spit us out reborn."

 We were all leaning forward, motionless. My mouth had fallen open; I was aware of every breath I took.

"And that, to me, is the terrible seduction of Dionysiac ritual. Hard for us to imagine. That pure fire of being." (TSH, p. 40)

APOLLO AND DIONYSUS

The epigraph that begins Book II of *The Secret History* is taken from a well-known text, E. R. Dodds's *The Greeks and the Irrational*, a book consisting of a series of lectures he gave in 1949 at the University of Berkeley, California. Tartt takes the epigraph from the third lecture, "The Blessings of Madness": "Dionysus [is] the Master of Illusions, who could make a vine grow out of a ship's plank, and in general enable his votaries to see the world as the world's not." The epigraph itself relates to a story, taken from Homer, in which Dionysus was captured by pirates and bound. But the ropes that bound him fell away, a vine grew around the mast, Dionysus turned into a lion and the pirates fell into the sea, whereupon they were turned into dolphins. It is another version of illusion and reality and a warning to those who cross Dionysus. Dodds's description of Dionysian revelry points to the source for Julian's discussion in *The Secret History*:

[Dionysus] is Lusios, "the Liberator"—the god who by very simple means, or by other means not so simple, enables you for a short time to *stop being yourself*, and thereby sets you free. That was, I think, the main secret of his appeal in the Archaic Age: not only because life in that age was often a thing to escape from, but more specifically because the individual, as the modern world knows him, began in that age to emerge for the first time from the old solidarity of the family, and found the unfamiliar burden of individual responsibility hard to bear. Dionysus could lift it from him. For Dionysus was the Master of Magical Illusions, who could make a vine grow out of a ship's plank, and in general enable his votaries to see the world as the world's not. As the Scythians in Herodotus put it, "Dionysus leads people on to behave madly"—which could mean anything from "letting yourself go" to becoming "possessed." The aim of his cult was *ecstasis*— which again could mean anything from "taking you out of yourself" to a profound alteration of personality. And its psychological function was to satisfy and relieve the impulse to reject responsibility, an impulse which exists in all of us and can become under certain social conditions an irresistible craving. (ER Dodds "The Blessings of Madness" in *The Greeks and the Irrational* pp. 76–77)

Dodds's description of the evolution of social practice and identity is suggestive of the social contexts and practices that are described in *The Secret History*: life in this age, like life in that age, seems still a thing that everyone wants to escape from—Henry, Richard, Judy Poovey, Cloke Rayburn, even Mrs. Corcoran with her vast supply of uppers and downers. In the modern age, however, while there is no longer the "solidarity of the family", the burden of individuality seems, still, hard to bear. Bunny's constant sponging seems like an abdication of responsibility, Camilla's acquiescence a giving up of individuality. Even Francis's decision to marry and retain his inheritance rather than to earn his own independent living and be cut off from what family he has is an abnegation of his individual responsibility out in the world. The past seems implicated in the present, and the ancient Greeks, in the event, seem to speak, not just to their own culture but also to something prevalent in "human nature." We don't learn from the past, in other words: we simply repeat it. All that is, apart from Richard, whose narrative in *The Secret History* is one that takes him towards a painful self-awareness.

Apollo was, amongst other things, the Greek god of healing, music, prophecy and light. Sometimes known as Apollo Lykeios, he is intimately connected with the Lyceum, teaching place of Aristotle in Ancient Greece, after which Julian Morrow names his own place of learning at Hampden. Dionysus, in Greek myth, is the god of wine and ecstasy (also known as the Roman god Bacchus). Although less benevolent than Apollo, he is also celebrated for being a giver of joy. The Dionysian experience, as we see in *The Secret History*, is felt through ecstasy and the transcendence of identity. But Julian does not warn his students that along with the promise of transcendence can also come the reality of violence, a violence which will be their undoing. Since they do not live in Ancient Greece, and they are not dramatic or mythological figures, and since no one is above the law, there must be a price to pay. And Dionysian worshippers were capable of savage acts of mutilation, as we see in both the *Bacchae* of Euripides and in *The Secret History*.

EURIPIDES: THE *BACCHAE*

To read the *Bacchae* is to enhance our own reading of *The Secret History*, to understand aspects of it differently or better. Euripides' *Bacchae* (bacchae were female followers of Dionysus) has been recognized as an important source for *The Secret History*. Dionysus, the divine son of Zeus and the mortal Semele, has returned to Thebes to enact revenge upon Agave, his mother's sister, for suggesting that Dionysus is fully mortal, not divine. He drives the women of Thebes mad with Dionysiac frenzy, and persuades Agave's son Pentheus to dress as a woman and spy on them. When the women see him, (an occurrence engineered by Dionysus) Agave mutilates and dismembers him, exacting the penalty for spying on bacchic rituals, (an action which is re-enacted by the group in the murder of the farmer). When Agave is released from her frenzy, she is made to realize that she has dismembered her own son, and is condemned to live her life in permanent exile.

François Pauw has noted that it is possible to read Tartt's novel as "a Greek tragedy in novel form." (Pauw, I, p. 149) Henry's description of the bacchanal in the forest remains faithful to the violence of Euripides's drama, from the frenzied excursion outside the conscious self to the sacrificial mutilation of the unwitting farmer, the violent brutality of whose death results from Henry's apparently superhuman strength during the ritual. But we already know that Henry is capable of feats requiring great strength since he broke the tough Spike Romney's collar bone: arguably, the ritual intensifies normality, but it does not change it. Since Henry would have been familiar with the *Bacchae*, one can only wonder that he did not think beforehand that Dionysus would demand a bloody sacrifice involving some of our most sacred cultural taboos. Camille

Paglia's forthright description of the *Bacchae* is suggestive of *The Secret History* itself: "Society in its late or decadent phase. The ruling hierarchy consists of the senile and the adolescent (i.e., Cadmus and Pentheus). Pentheus is like Homer's callow suitors, a lost generation of pampered dandies unseasoned by war and adventure."[3] Certainly the inept Dr. Roland and his friend, the antique Dr. Blind, the paranoid Georges Laforgue, together with Jud the "Party Pig" and his friend Frank (who are immune to censure because both their fathers are on the board of directors at Hampden, (TSH, p. 355)) constitute a hierarchy of the senile and the adolescent.

But resonances of plot and ritual aside, the self-conscious theatricality of the play also speaks to the self-conscious literariness and theatricality of Tartt's novel. Since Dionysus, or the Dionysian, is so crucial to events in the novel, I want to suggest that Dionysus's function as god of Athenian theatre is also important to an understanding of one of the techniques of *The Secret History*. For although this is an admittedly entrancing and engaging book, we can achieve Henry's desire, and "lose ourselves" in it, our attention is also frequently drawn towards the fact that we are reading a literary text. Why?

PERFORMANCE AND THEATRICALITY

The *Bacchae* also draws attention to its own theatricality, to its own spectacle as performance as we watch characters consciously and deliberately don their costumes and play a part which is not, so to speak, their own: the Theban women have been driven to live in the mountain "in a state of violent delusion . . . forced . . . to wear the trappings of my rites"; Dionysus has transformed his own appearance from god to man, and Pentheus is persuaded to dress as a woman in order to spy on the bacchantes. To watch the *Bacchae* is to witness a play about performance.

This framing device is replicated within Richard's narrative, when he occasionally steps back from the action. On one occasion, during the hunt for Bunny, he imagines what they'd typically be doing if they were in a film: *"if this was a movie we'd all be fidgeting and acting really suspicious."* (TSH, p. 308) Indeed, if it ever becomes a movie, perhaps this is what they *will* be doing. Stepping out of the fictional frame by imagining the scene as fiction lends some credibility to their thwarted "simple tale", now fast becoming an epic (at one point, Julian and Henry appreciate the aesthetic quality of the snowy landscape crowded with people looking for Bunny because it reminds them both of Tolstoy.) Later Julian says to Richard "Life has got awfully dramatic all of a sudden, hasn't it? Just like a fiction . . ." (TSH, p. 328). Indeed, Richard can only think of the murder as though it was a film, seen through anyone else's eyes but his own. He refers to the farmer as a "prop", and refers to Bunny as cast "in the tragic role." And when Julian finally discovers the truth about the farmer and Bunny, Richard notes, *pace The Wizard of Oz*, that "the charming theatrical curtain had dropped away" (TSH, p. 477), revealing the reality behind the illusion or artifice that Julian had created for them. Moreover, Camilla becomes inscrutable to Richard in the end, because he realizes that "she was such an expert actress" (TSH, p. 381). The group themselves are forced to assume roles which they are constantly in danger of dropping, both during and after Bunny's funeral. Charles, in particular, feels as though he's acting a part during the police investigation. And Richard comes to realize that under Julian's careful *Magus*-like tutelage they have all been persuaded to play roles. And while once he found this "magnificent" since it released him from a past which he found anyway "disposable as a plastic cup", experience also teaches him that there are other, more sinister ways to regard the donning of masks and the adoption of personae.

In the end, he realizes that his assumed character now defines him, as the imitation takes over the original: "I had more or less become the character which for a long time I had so skilfully played . . ." (TSH, p. 305) But role playing is widespread in the book, reaching beyond an enactment of Greek Tragedy to the televisual culture of modern America, and the book's embrace of high and popular forms of culture emphasizes the similarity between the two. The local news reporter Liz Ocavello leans her arm "Oprah-style" on the beleaguered Palestinian-American (TSH, p. 343) as Bill Hundy leans forward in his mock-Shaker chair prior to introducing chaos into her carefully orchestrated chat-show. How do they meet the chaos? They smoothly switch to commercial breaks featuring that great symbol of Corporate America: McDonalds. Now we know where we are. The Corcoran clan remind Richard of the Kennedy family (Mrs. Corcoran even wears "faux-Jackie" glasses" TSH, pp. 392–3) and Bunny's funeral reminds him of the motorcade at John Kennedy's funeral, as though images supersede actual experience. To Richard, Judy Poovey's friend Tracy behaves like Mary Tyler Moore, and Sophie Dearbold looks like Audrey Hepburn. Few people are seen or judged outside one or another, classical or popular, frame of reference; in their postmodern world, the image becomes more real than the real. Even the final epigraph of the novel seems to underline this: "He look'd not like the ruins of his youth/But like the ruins of those ruins." These imitations, or simulacra, are prevalent everywhere: from the nineteenth century imitation of classicism at Francis's country house and Richard's experience of "memories of things I'd never known." (TSH, p. 74) Even some of the critical evaluations of the novel echo this narrative habit whereby a thing is experienced or perceived via reference only to something else: "The atmosphere that Hampden evokes," suggests François Pauw, "is redolent of John Irving, Robin Williams' *Dead Poets Society*, and *The Great Gatsby*."[4] All our cultural references, then, are entangled and confused in each other, suggesting that there is nothing new we can do or be. It's the imitation, the ersatz or pretend world that Henry would like to escape. At the country house, he likes to get up very early in the morning because "morning light can make the most vulgar things tolerable." (TSH, p. 79)

Authentic experience is shown to be only ever imitative. Even Henry and Camilla's description of their bacchanal sounds like something they'd already read in Euripides. Charles and Camilla weren't "carnal" *because* of the ritual: their relationship was sexual anyway, the bacchanal only exacerbated and intensified what was already present. Henry's account of the bacchanal demonstrates the impossibility of achieving what he desires: for to remember and describe the event is to render the primitive sensible. He understands himself only as it has already been made legibly available to him. Like Richard, he has memories of things he's never known.

DETECTIVES IN *THE SECRET HISTORY*

Towards the end of his narrative, Richard tells us that he reads Dickens's *Our Mutual Friend* (1865) to Francis, then recuperating after his attempted suicide. Adrian Poole has observed that in this book, Dickens created a new kind of murderer in Bradley Headstone, the school teacher, one "whose violence is masked by a veneer of decency . . ."[5], raising the unsettling possibility, as Martin Swales has put it, that "Civilisation may house barbarity within its wall." The densely plotted *Our Mutual Friend* is detective fiction of sorts, and its muted appearance at the end of *The Secret History* intimates that this is also how we might regard *The Secret History* — as detective fiction of sorts.

The false leads and dead ends during the hunt for Bunny are part of the specific appeal of Tartt's well-paced narrative, boxing clever with what *we* know and what we cannot possibly know or expect to happen next (viz. the kidnapping and drug dealing sub-plots). One of the appeals of detective fiction is that it restores order where there had been chaos — wrongs tend to be righted and justice prevails. Indeed, Tartt herself has argued that this is one of the functions of the novel: "Something in the spirit longs for meaning — longs to believe in a world order where nothing is purposeless ... The novel can provide this kind of synthesis in microcosm ..."[6] And yet this novel doesn't.

Richard's narrative is an attempt to take control of a story (the murder of Bunny) which is about loss of control (the unforeseen delay in recovering his body). Of course, *really* it is framed by Tartt's very tightly managed plot structure, so loss of control is actually a well-staged illusion. But control and its loss, or order and chaos, reverberate continuously through the novel. We hear about order and chaos in Richard's first seminar with Julian, a discussion which functions as the supposed inspiration for the subsequent bacchanal, the purpose of which is to lose control of the self. We see Bunny spiraling out of control both psychologically and then tragically as he drops to his death. The sprawl of Bunny's body at the bottom of the ravine is meant to be read and interpreted as "a tale that told itself simply and well", though in this simple scenario, *we* know that appearance and reality are actually horribly dislocated. But the untimely snowfall opens up the efficient tale to one of torturous suspense leavened with comic misreading as it mutates into a detective murder-mystery on an epic scale, involving local and state police, the FBI, college administrators, boy scouts, maintenance workers, security guards, Hampden students, great swathes of towns-people, a psychic, a fingerprint expert and a team of dogs. To the numb horror of the group, who can only stand by and act accord-ingly (and acting is precisely what they do), Bunny's supposed walking accident turns into a suspected international kidnapping by Arabs. The other possibility that the police work with is that Bunny has been despatched by desperate New York drug dealers. As events follow their grim and artless trajectory they seem to mock the very things that the group loved best about Greek: ". . . a language ob-sessed with action, action marching relentlessly ahead and with yet more actions filing in from either side to fall into neat step at the rear, in a long straight rank of cause and effect toward what will be inevitable, the only possible end." (TSH, p. 189)

The detective genre also often requires "a setting which is not just an enclosed world but also a world of high sophistication."[7] The location of the campus setting is important, since it offers a realistic base which stabilizes this occasionally fantastical narrative, as well as an enclosed world apart from the casual violence that seems to have such a skulking presence in this region of Vermont: Richard, lost on the way to Leo the hippie's warehouse during the Christmas vacation, hesitates at the door of the Boulder Tap and baulks at the last moment: ". . . it was the epicenter of what little crime there was in Hampden—knifings, rapes, never a single wit-ness." (TSH, p. 106) Thus the civilized world and the criminal world, or, put another way, the world of order and the world of chaos lock horns. So far, so good.

Arguably, though, *The Secret History* unsettles the rules of the murder-mystery by drawing attention to a different relationship be-tween the order that the law upholds and the chaos that the transgressor or criminal seeks to accomplish. The balance of appear-ance and reality is crucial to this relationship: as Charles says during the hunt for Bunny: "I never realized, you know, how much we rely on appearances . . . It's not that we're smart, it's just that we don't *look* like we did it." (TSH, p. 322) When the local and state police descend upon Hampden in search of the missing Bunny, Tartt, as we know, frustrates the simple tale that Henry had planned for Bunny's epitaph, and instead she stages a series of unexpected twists, attributing different sinister motives to Bunny's mysterious disappearance. These unexpected twists, which constitute much of the novel's suspense, reinforce the sense that actually no one is in control, and the figures of authority we might traditionally look to (parents, teachers, police) are either absent, bad, dead, senile or incompetent. After all, in the end the police unwittingly *side* with the transgressor: even when Henry tries to introduce another aspect into the case, asking whether the FBI think that Bunny killed himself, they reject the suggestion, preferring to accept the interpretation that Henry had intended all along: Bunny's death looks like an unfortunate hiking accident, therefore it must *be* one. And the ones who *are* punished by the law (Cloke Rayburn, Laura Stora) have been caught for entirely unrelated crimes. But as we know, in *The Secret History* transgression begets transgression and only the *illusion* of order is ever restored.

BUNNY CORCORAN: BOY DETECTIVE

Agents Davenport and Sciola aren't the only detectives in the novel. Apart from Julian, who unintentionally solves the crime and then hands the letter back before abandoning his protegé (there's more to punishment than incarceration), Richard and Bunny also serve their time as functional detective figures. At one point, Henry grimly refers to Bunny as "Bunny Corcoran, Boy Detective" (TSH, p. 168) after Francis imagines him as the figure who gives the game away in the Perry Mason program (perhaps this is where he thinks

Bunny really belongs?). But in a world where order is sunk in chaos, the Boy Detective is himself deeply compromised: his outrage at the bacchanal isn't a moral one, at least in the beginning, and not consciously anyway: he's furious at having been left out. But law and order are seriously compromised when the murderer's next victim is the detective figure, who doesn't so much arrive at the scene of the crime as constitute it. Richard, sunk in confusion by the apparent disappearance of the others on a one way flight to Argentina, goes home and reads Raymond Chandler (which one? *The Long Goodbye? Farewell My Lovely?*), a detective whose fiction is distinguished by the fact that "the subject whose truth the detective is in search of is the detective himself."[8] Richard achieves insight only towards the end of his narrative:

He had appealed to my vanity, allowing me to think I'd figured it out for myself . . . and I had congratulated myself in the glow of his praise, when in fact—I saw this now, I'd been too vain to see it then—he'd led me right to it, coaxing and flattering all the way. (TSH, p. 459)

And so the criminal outsmarts the detective before recruiting him as an indispensable accessory to his next crime, as Richard sadly, slowly realizes, too long after the event. This scene draws attention to themes like illusion and reality, or it helps us to map the path of Richard's disillusionment or allows us to assess the extent and nature of Henry's evil which is becoming more visible. But perhaps we can also expand this, and think about it in terms of the bigger questions that Tartt raises about her portrayal of an atrophied contemporary culture. The detective has insight into the depravities of the human condition, but in Tartt's novel they either don't want to see it (Davenport and Sciola, even Julian, who just wants his name kept out of potential scandal) or they cannot keep order and chaos apart, since they collude with criminal opportunity. In their new world of inverted values, the sublime is replaced with the ridiculous: the "divine" Julian, representative of the ancient culture Henry so venerates, is substituted with his antithesis, Dick Spence, young and newly married: "*Agathon*. Do you know how I remember that word? 'Agatha Christie writes good mysteries.'" (TSH, p. 488) Well, perhaps the order is not so inverted after all: Agatha Christie is what does for them all in the end. After that, the game seems up. Richard stands outside the Lyceum listening to Henry and Charles arguing "*Who is in control here?* I thought, dismayed." (TSH, p. 489)

NIETZSCHE'S HEIR

The Apollonian and the Dionysian, though apparently antagonistic, require one another to maintain a creative equilibrium. Julian says as much when he warns against becoming one or the other—either utterly ascetic and intellectual, or utterly pleasure seeking. Henry seems central to this formulation. On the one hand, he seems opposed to the Dionysian. His learning is upheld throughout the book: although Bunny parodies Henry's scholarly bent, he comments during his drunken lunch with Richard that you couldn't beat Henry away from Greek with a stick. But Henry learns for the sake of learning. His project is to study "the 12 Great Cultures", but this seems redolent of "a culture of dry scholarship, dedicated to amassing and cataloguing the achievements of the past."[9] In other words, since there is nothing dynamic or regenerative about Henry's learning, we might conclude that he represents an aspect of that other moribund world that he encounters every day at Hampden. Douglas Smith has commented that for Friedrich Nietzsche, this kind of culture and learning "offers a parallel with the German culture of his day—overly historicist and anxious to imitate and collect the forms of the past rather than to develop a vital contemporary culture."[10] On the other hand, what also drives Henry is his desire to re-embrace the myth that Julian talks about during that first seminar, to transcend the isolation (perceived as a burden) of the self and achieve transcendence: in other words, he feels the pull of the Dionysian. Once he has succumbed to it and successfully performed the rite, once he has murdered the farmer, he changes, as we see. Henry thus seems like a descendant of Nietzsche:

The ecstasy of the Dionysian state, with its annihilation of the usual limits and borders of existence, contains for its duration a *lethargic* element in which all past personal experience is submerged. And so this chasm of oblivion separates the world of everyday reality from that of Dionysian reality. However, as soon as that everyday reality returns to consciousness, it is experienced for what it is with disgust: an ascetic mood which negates the will is the fruit of those conditions. (*The Birth of Tragedy*, p. 46)

Although his desire to leave the burden of selfhood behind is fostered in the first place by his worship of Julian, and his fascination with and love of Greek literature and culture, Henry comes to believe himself to be above morality:

"The world has always been an empty place to me. I was incapable of enjoying even the simplest things. I felt dead in everything I did." He brushed the dirt from his hands. "But then it changed," he said. "The night I killed that man."

[. . .] "It was the most important night of my life," he said calmly. (TSH, p. 463)

And he goes on to assert that he's achieved his aim, which is to live without thinking. Since this seems to equate to a joyless and apparently mechanical existence, this seems puzzling. His behavior before, during and after Bunny's death reveals a progression of sorts as he both closes himself off morally and opens himself up (immorally?) to the implications of his actions. In fact Henry seems to be the heir of Friedrich Nietzsche, becoming a sort of Nietzschean *ubermensch* or superman who believes that, ". . . it is no longer the consequences but the origin of an action that one allows to decide its value." (*Beyond Good and Evil*, p. 44)

Although Henry is responsible for the mutilation of the farmer, the group all seem oddly unmoved by their experience. Partly, this seems like a process of disavowal, a refusal to countenance what they have done. Francis feels "awfully embarassed" by the farmer's death and thinks that Richard's "being so nice" about it. Richard's empathy with the others about Bunny's ability to make them uncomfortable seems strange: he notes Bunny's teasing him about whether or not there's polyester blend in his shirt, or whether the cut in his pants was a "Western cut", but actually the comparison between this and his taunting of the others is bizarre. Being badgered about the lies he tells about which school he went to is hardly in the same league as being harassed about a murder you've committed, but they seem to share equal space in Richard's mind, as though all constitute equally good reasons for wanting to see the end of Bunny.

BUNNY'S FUNERAL

The funeral is a mixture of the comic and the absurd, as the avuncular Mr. Corcoran alternates between remembering and forgetting his grief. Although Henry hates the Corcorans, Francis is clearly touched by Mr. Corcoran's friendliness towards him. After a long and comic exchange over Sophie Dearbold's lineage:

"Why your *aunt*, honey. Your daddy's sister. That pretty Jean Lickfold . . ."
"No, sir. *Dear*bold.
"Dearfold. Well, isn't that strange . . ." (TSH, p. 364)

And so on, until, to their consternation, he bursts into tears and wails his lachrymose sentiments: "Honey, how are we going to get along without him?" (TSH, p. 364) As Francis and Richard help him to a chair, he grabs Richard by the wrist and looks at him helplessly, and this for Richard is the first moment of realization:

Suddenly, and for the first time, really, I was struck by the bitter, irrevocable truth of it; the evil of what we had done. It was like running full speed into a brick wall. I let go his collar, feeling completely helpless. (TSH, p. 365)

And yet Tartt strikes an uneven tone in these passages: the dawning of Richard's guilty realization of what he has colluded with is counterbalanced with Cloke catching Richard coming out of the bathroom with Camilla, or the raid on Mrs. Corcoran's drug supplies followed by Mrs. Corcoran's discovery of the theft, ". . . the missing items were small things, of sentimental value, and of no use to anyone but herself." TSH, p. 397) Cloke, Charles and Bram Rooney smoking pot outside is counterbalanced with Mrs. Corcoran's choosing to see, or again, not to hear that Brandon's Uncle Bunny once called him a bastard, and so on.[11] These pre-funeral scenes appear to satirize the vanities and values of the kind of America that the Corcoran family represent and embody, and they also represent a change in direction for the narrative, which now shifts to a consideration of guilt and the final dissolution of the apparently water-tight group. In a text that continuously haunts itself, Mrs. Corcoran can be found inspecting ferns, unwittingly mimicking the scene that preceded her son's final moments. Though the irony is not remarked on by Richard, it is, nonetheless, there; and at moments like this, the authorial narrative seems drained of all sympathy for her. Mrs. Corcoran's sense of place seems utterly *out* of place as she prepares for Bunny's funeral, from her inspection of the floral wreaths and tributes ("This African violet is almost dead. Louise would be humiliated if she knew." TSH, p. 367) to her small talk with Francis ("I was so sorry when I heard she'd been admitted to the Betty Ford Center." TSH, p. 368) Just as unsettling is Mr. Corcoran's attempts at conversation with Henry: "What you boys been doing up there all afternoon . . . Looking at girlie magazines?" (TSH, p. 368) Also misplaced seems Marion's grief, as she is chiefly upset about the fact that Sophie Dearbold, an old crush of Bunny's, has been invited to the funeral. (TSH, p. 371) Tartt hams up the general awfulness of the situation—Mr. Corcoran's sentimental (and inadvertently rude) recollections of Bunny's first meeting with Henry, his innocuous recapitulation of Bunny's ill-tempered plans for the summer, and so on. Comic routines are sustained in the build up to the funeral and the day of the funeral itself, subverting the piety and solemnity of the occasion, and unveiling the hypocrisy of the family. Thus we can never be sure whether their behaviour is a manifestation of grief or an affectation of grief as they swiftly recollect themselves from jollity to mourning to jollity again, as though they are defined only by their public and outer lives, a mask for their spiritual and emotional sterility. (Observe Mr. Corcoran's abrupt shift from sorrow, as he places his son's coffin in the hearse, to his sudden gamboling across the lawn to meet Mr. Vanderfeller, the man whose grandfather has an interest in the stock of Mr. Corcoran's bank. (TSH, pp. 391–2)) Or we might pause to reflect where Mrs. Corcoran's true values really lie as she disciplines two of her grandsons: "You ought to be sitting quietly somewhere thinking about all the nice things he used to do for you instead of running around and scuffing up this pretty new floor that Grandmother just had refurnished." (TSH, p. 387)

The poses sustained by the group themselves are fast beginning to crumble. Charles drives off in Francis's car, with the roof down in the rain. Francis's occasional peevishness is again apparent as they squabble over whether Francis has ever driven with the top down in the rain or not, Camilla is irritated because her favorite umbrella blows away immediately after the funeral service. Such petty trivialities seem odd in the context of the occasion, but they are also perhaps necessary reminders for the group of their ordinary routines, immersed as they are in the extraordinary outcome of their own handiwork. But it's at Bunny's funeral that the signs of their guilty disturbance first become really manifest; and guilt, it seems, is the only authentic emotion felt at the funeral.

After Henry had scrambled up the ravine to confirm that Bunny was dead, he had wiped dirt on his trousers. In a scene which has been much admired by critics and reviewers, Henry, after throwing earth onto Bunny's coffin ". . . with terrible composure, . . . stepped back and absently dragged the hand across his chest, smearing mud upon his lapel, his tie, the starched immaculate white of his shirt." (TSH, p. 395) François Pauw has found this "one of the most shocking passages in the novel" but also one of the most revealing:

This is nothing but ritual defilement, the besmirching of the suit symbolizing the uncleansed *miasma* of the soul. Thus, even Henry, the least scrupulous of the guilty foursome, betrays his remorse most vividly.[12]

AFTER THE FUNERAL

Afterwards, like Dante, Richard feels as though "I had just come back from the brink of Death itself, back to the sun and air." (TSH, pp. 404–5) But the apparent restoration of normality and order is, from this stage on, followed quickly by its usurpation. On a drunkenly cheery visit to Henry, he notices that he's planted the fern he'd dug up prior to pushing Bunny over the edge of the ravine. (TSH, p. 405) Later that night Richard is called to take Francis to hospital. Since there's nothing physically wrong with him, the Doctor asks him whether he feels afraid "For no good reason you can think of?" (TSH, p. 409) Charles and Camilla tell Richard not to mention Francis's panic attack to Henry, as though they are afraid of him. Again, the illusion of order is momentarily restored during an evening at Charles and Camilla's, until Richard realizes that the broken mirror, one of the talking points of the evening, wasn't an accident, as Charles had claimed, since Richard can see that someone had thrown a highball glass with great force at it. (TSH, p. 413) Or when Henry sends Richard to town to bail Charles out of his drunk driving escapade, he realizes "how poorly I had been apprized of the situation I was heading into. Henry hadn't told me a thing." (TSH, p. 414) Again, Henry asks Richard to look after the matter, to be there at 9:00 for the court hearing. (TSH, p. 417) When Henry suggests that he's not asking that much of Richard, he also realizes *"Only that I do what you tell me . . ."* (TSH, p. 418) As Charles and Richard walk along the highway back to Hampden, chinks in the façade of their friendship with Henry begin to appear: Charles tells Richard that he's tired of Henry telling him what to do, Richard is beginning to wonder why they do what he says. (TSH, p. 420) But more than this, Charles is beginning to blame him for engineering the murder, the bacchanal and his own encounters with the police. And as the events of the narrative come to their conclusion, another reading is pried open for us, one that produces Henry as a cynical manipulator, the others as his unwitting dupes, opening up the narrative to a study of the seduction of a group of innocents into evil. Richard's retrospectively told narrative retraces the stages of that seduction, "to arrive where we started/ And know the place for the first time."

INTERTEXTS IN *THE SECRET HISTORY*

The Secret History is made up of other books. References and allusions to other literary works (both "high" and "popular") are liberally sprinkled throughout Richard's narrative. Towards the beginning of this section I suggested that books make sense of books; they're not, after all, produced in a vacuum irrespective of the cultural influences that shape their writers and their readers. Comparing a text with another one by the same author, or according to the criteria of a genre, is often how we begin to evaluate and measure a text. Books also bear witness to the presence and influence of whatever the author has read, but also, importantly, of whatever it is that *we* read too. And while our readings of *The Secret History* will no doubt overlap (since it's likely that groups of us share common cultural assumptions), no two readings are ever exactly the same, since we bring our individual experiences to bear on our reading practices. What are all these literary references and allusions doing in this text, and do they matter?

In *Our Mutual Friend* Betty Higden, who has taken in an orphaned child called Sloppy, says "You mightn't think it, but Sloppy is a beautiful reader of a newspaper. He do the Police in different voices." T. S. Eliot (whose influence on Tartt has been well noted) had used "He do the Police in different voices" as a working title-cum-epigraph for his poem, *The Wasteland* (1922). Tartt's novel makes overt reference to *The Wasteland* (TSH, p. 77), as well as implicit reference. Thus, she quotes explicitly from the poem, and she also makes use of some of the references that Eliot himself used, such as the *Upanishads* which Henry reads (presumably for consolation) at Bunny's funeral. Also referred to in her novel is F. Scott Fitzgerald's *The Great Gatsby* (TSH, p. 68) which Richard claims is his favorite novel, identifying as he does with Jay Gatsby (rather than the book's narrator, Nick Carraway, perhaps a more obvious point of comparison).

The Great Gatsby and *The Wasteland* constitute part of the canonical fabric of European and Anglo-American literary Modernism (a term used to designate experimental development in the arts between the two World Wars). Both texts gesture towards a post-war malaise and dearth of spiritual value in the contemporary cultures and relationships that they document, but *The Wasteland* in particular is made up of fragments of other texts, and in common with *The Secret History*, alludes to *The Inferno, Purgatorio*, Jacobean dramatists, and the *Upanishads*, the philosophical treatises which conclude the sacred Hindu Veda. Eliot and Fitzgerald provide clear literary antecedents for Tartt's late twentieth-century text, helping to establish a literary pedigree for it that stretches way beyond the "Brat Pack" novels of the 1980s, as well as supporting the thematic concerns of her novel, one of which is an implicit recognition that what we know and how we perceive people, events, *things*, is through a web of cultural signs which are complicated and implicated in each other.

Tartt's acknowledgement to her editor, Gary Fisketjohn, echoes Eliot's dedication of *The Wasteland* to *his* editor, Ezra Pound: "*il miglior fabbrio*", or "to the better craftsman." (In *The Secret History* Julian Morrow is reputed to have been the friend of both Eliot and Pound, TSH, p. 17) *Il miglior fabbrio* is, in turn, borrowed from Dante's *Purgatorio*, a work which Henry holds in his hand as he discusses poisoning Bunny. Like Eliot, Tartt also borrows from Dante's *Inferno*. Dante's circles of hell reverberate through Tartt's novel, from the opening of Canto I, where the dark wood symbolizes Dante's losing his spiritual way, to his being invited to join the five select poets of antiquity to the rocky ravine that signals the seventh circle of Hell. There's also, Henry would certainly have known, a place for suicides in the Sixth Circle.

Eliot, we know, did not keep his title/epigraph to *The Wasteland* from *Our Mutual Friend*. He opted instead for this, taken from *The Satyricon* (AD 63–5) of Petronius. Trimalchio, addressing Agammenon, says:

And as for the Sibyl, I saw her with my own eyes at Cumae, suspended in a bottle, and when the boys asked her, "Sibyl, what is your wish?" she would reply, "I want to die."

As legend has it, Apollo had offered her anything she wished in return for love. She asked to live as many years as there were grains of sand in a pile of sweepings (or in her hand, versions differ), but she forgot to ask for continued youth as well — hence her wish to die. *The Satyricon* is an explicitly-told series of sexual and inebriate adventures, the interpretation of which seems to change according to the cultural or moral sensibilities of whichever era reads it. Eliot's choice of this fragment of speech, taken from the gluttonous figure of Trimalchio, has, for example, persuaded critics to view the work as a moral critique of a corrupt society, "of sensuality without joy, satiety without fulfilment, degradation without grief and horror . . ."[13], all of which Eliot rehearses in his poem, and which are characteristic of *The Secret History* and of its often-cited predecessors: *Less Than Zero; The Rules of Attraction; American Psycho; Bright Lights, Big City*. (Another passage in *The Satyricon* contains some relevance to Tartt's novel: "Asclytus had buried his head in his cloak; he doubtless remembered the warning that it was dangerous to witness the secret rites of others." (*The Satyricon*, p. 14))

Trimalchio in West Egg was one of Fitzgerald's abandoned titles for the book that became *The Great Gatsby*, Richard's favorite novel. (TSH, p. 68) When he tries to re-read it, he sees only a correlation between his own and Jay Gatsby's ill-fated life, although Tartt conceived of *Gatsby* as relevant to her novel in a more generalized sense. *Gatsby* helps to define some of the broader issues which Tartt explores: the self-invention of the naïve suburban figure, the transition from humble to stellar social orbits (also a plot element in *Our Mutual Friend*), the adoration of excessive material wealth (also *Our Mutual Friend*), the disowning of parents. And as in *Gatsby*, money is at the root of *The Secret History*: new money, old money, no money, all of which will be instrumental in their respective attractions, corruption and ruin.

As some reviewers noted, Bunny shares his nickname with the critic, Edmund Wilson. In *Axel's Castle* a collection of essays first published in 1931, Wilson's contribution on T. S. Eliot also throws some light on *The Secret History*. For example, at one point, Wilson compares Eliot with Gustave Flaubert, the author of another text which is cited in *The Secret History*, *Madame Bovary*, and which has in common with Tartt's novel its eponymous bored and provincial figure who is in love with the prestige of material wealth. It's tempting to speculate that when Camilla finds the greyhound it's done only to engineer a comparison with Emma Bovary. Wilson's comparison of Eliot with Flaubert speaks to one of the central concerns of *The Secret History*: "Eliot, like Flaubert, feels at every turn that human life is now ignoble, sordid or tame, and he is haunted and tormented by intimations that it has once been otherwise."[14] His comments on *The Wasteland* seem apposite, then: "The poet of 'The Wasteland' is living half the time in the real world of contemporary London and half the time in the haunted wilderness of the medieval legend."[15] At least, it seems apposite in relation to one scene that Richard remembers from his happier days with the group. He's in a boat with Henry and Camilla. Henry is talking about Elizabeth I and the Earl of Leicester. Years later, says Richard, he recognizes the scene, but in a different context, and he goes on to cite a portion of "The Fire Sermon", Part Three of *The Wasteland*, Eliot's own densely allusive poem:

> *Elizabeth and Leicester*
> *Beating oars*
> *The stern was formed*
> *A gilded shell*
> *Red and Gold*
>   (TSH, p. 77)

One of Richard's occasional habits as a narrator is to interject a phrase or allusion to or from another text, sometimes from his own vapid journal, or in this case from Eliot. Since he always assumes a self-evident significance, the quotation tends to be left unexplained, and we have to do the work. This particular allusion seems poised somewhere between the languorous days of *Brideshead Revisited* and the *Wasteland,* itself a fragmentary poem that resists narrative coherence and which is built on the remains of both the ancient and modern worlds. (Harold Acton, the Oxford aesthete who's mentioned as disliking Julian), was said to have recited *The Wasteland* through a megaphone, just as Anthony Blanche does in *Brideshead* p. 42) In a sense, Richard's own narrative re-writes or overwrites the meaning of the original text by snapping out of context scenes and phrases of his choosing, rehabilitating specific textual moments within this new literary context and offering a new meaning with the new novel as new host. Like the detective hunt for Bunny's body, these allusions may well be nothing more than red herrings, positioning the reader or critic as detective, and, as happens with Agents Davenport and Sciola, out-foxing us all. At one point in his essay, Edmund Wilson parodies Eliot: "At this rate . . . we should have to read the whole of literature in order to appreciate a single book, and Eliot fails to supply us with a reason why we should go to the trouble of doing so."[16] Of course, we don't need to have read the whole of literature to appreciate *The Secret History* but we might question what it's doing there. In the case of this citation from *The*

Wasteland, the literary text reminds Richard of the supposedly extra-textual event that he now narrates: Henry rowing him and Camilla in a boat, with Henry talking about Elizabeth and Leicester. We can choose to read it in any number of ways: perhaps it's of no thematic significance, and supports the realist nature of the narrative, drawing attention to the co-incidence of Eliot's poem and Henry's conversation. Since co-incidence and chance function in such crucial ways to plot development in the novel, perhaps this is merely a textual echo of those themes, the chance finding of the poem jogging an earlier memory. But the quotation also draws attention to one of the big issues of the book: public and private history, the official history and the secret history. One important narrative, that of Elizabeth I as Virgin Queen, is offset against another, more scurrilous one: Elizabeth as the lover of the Earl of Leicester.

The book's title, as with so much else in it, is allusive. It is borrowed from the Byzantine historian Procopius (c. AD 500-after 562), the Emperor Justinian's official war historian. Procopius added to his official eight book *History of the Wars of Justinian* (527–53) with *Secret History*, a book that gives the off-the-record account which is critical of Justinian and casts gossipy aspersions on the morals of his wife, the Empress Theodora. And so while the additional book emphasizes the difference between official appearance and unofficial or hidden reality, it also throws into confusion quite where illusion and reality lie: which, now, is the "real" history, the one we are to believe? On what basis do we make our choices? Or does the existence of both just complicate what had seemed a simple enough division?

CONCLUSIONS

There are no moral absolutes in the world that Tartt creates in her novel; the narrative takes occasional glimpses at the world outside Hampden, but the group recoil from the latent violence and racism that they see to their cost: ignoring it doesn't make it go away, and makes them blind to the fact that they replicate the modern world they so disdain. Arguably, Henry's *hauteur* renders him isolated; it's difficult to see what intellectual companionship he derives from the others who tend to defer to his superior learning. His austere pursuit of learning for its own sake (like the creatively barren exercise of translating Milton into Latin) makes him partly the heir of Marlowe's *Dr. Faustus* who, bored with his books, sells his soul for 24 years of pleasure and then is invited to watch the Furies at work in Hell, "tossing damnèd souls/On burning forks"[17] before being physically mutilated by devils as a prelude to the eternal damnation of his soul. (In the Epilogue, Richard explicitly compares Henry to Faustus, TSH, p. 513)

Even the glimpses that are revealed within Hampden make Henry's quest seem more understandable, if Judy, Laura, Cloke, Bram, Jud and Frank constitute the identity of creative liberal American youth. Filtered through Richard's remembrances, which in turn are filtered through the intrigues of the Jacobean world stage, moral perspectives shift. Tartt may have seduction and guilt as the two thematic devices of her novel, but there is perhaps another question that the specific context of the Hampden world prompts: to echo Nietzsche, "What is the meaning of—morality?"[18] Although Richard feels some compunction at Bunny's funeral, it's for what they've done to Bunny's family, who themselves are wrapped up in the appearance of the thing rather than in grief at the loss of their youngest son. Henry's dutiful sacrifice at the novel's end is symptomatic, perhaps, of the failure of much: of the desire to return to myth and the failure of myth as an alternative to the deathly culture he has inherited. For as Nietzsche has it, the return to myth from cultural sterility has much to offer:

... were there perhaps in the centuries when the Greek body flourished, when the Greek soul bubbled over with life, such things as endemic raptures? Visions and hallucinations shared by entire communities, entire cult assemblies?[19]

What, after all, does the book say? Pauw suggests that "it holds a mirror to the nihilism of our time by employing an antithesis that has not lost any of its topicality, viz. that of the Apollonian vs. the Dionysian."[20] Certainly, *The Secret History* often seems as though it's structured on a series of binary oppositions: Apollo vs. Dionysus; order vs. chaos; barbarity vs. civilization; the world of learning vs. a world of ignorance; repression vs. hedonism; law vs. anarchy; the noble old world vs. the vacuous modern world, evil vs. good; Julian Morrow vs. Dick Spence. Richard's narrative is sometimes a flawed one: "I am unable to recall", "I honestly can't remember", "I don't think I can explain", "Even today I do not fully understand", "I wish I could remember more of what was said that day." These failures are iterated frequently in his narrative, exposing either his fallibility or his refusal to remember what is still too painful, adding a kind of verisimilitude or authenticity to his narrative. But his inability to remember, his constant forgetting, also honors an important aspect of this novel, and this is to do with human limitation, and the inability, as Julian had told them, to ever really know one another, or, indeed, ourselves. When he is not in the process of forgetting (or repressing) he tells us his dreams. The dream, as Freud tells us, is the "royal road to the unconscious", that repository of our un-wanted thoughts and feelings, the ones that are too difficult to manage or bear. *The Secret History* has two stories that, Richard says, tell themselves simply: Bunny's body at the bottom of the ravine and, at the end, Henry's suicide. "The story at the Albermarle was simple, it told itself, really" says Richard (TSH, p. 511) It is the secret history all over again, dramatizing the discrepancy between what really happened and what appears to have happened. Of course, stories don't just "tell themselves": in doing the reading, we also do the telling; we are the ones who animate plot, character, event, we decide where the emphasis lies. In the case of both the simple stories, the death of Bunny and the shooting at the Albermarle, Henry as the author of the drama (as Richard refers to him in the case of Bunny) is clearly not in control in terms of how those stories are read and interpreted: their meaning changes according to who's doing the reading, according to what perspective you want to prioritize. On the night of the murder, Richard, high on Demerol, thinks that Jud, the "Party Pig" now looks like a King from Irish legend, sporting a Burger King crown; the campus crowd he had once dismissed (*Hoi Polloi, Barbaroi*) he now sees as genial and benign. They're not different, but Richard is. In other words, nothing has a reliable or stable meaning, rather, interpretation is contingent upon where you happen to position yourself.

At the end of the novel, Richard recounts a dream in which Henry appears to him. The landscape of the dream seems partly inspired by Eliot's descriptions of the "Unreal City" in part I of *The Wasteland*, "The Burial of the Dead" in which the dead (borrowed by Eliot from *Inferno*) return and walk again. The post-war apocalyptic city seems like another of Richard's borrowed memories, as does its futuristic sci-fi regeneration. Yet his vision of the future is haunted by remnants of the past, as representations of the contemporary and the ancient world sit side by side: the laboratory in which, one assumes, new scientific discoveries will be made, the museum in which artefacts from the past are saved. The dream seems deliberately open-ended, replete with symbols of divinity, royalty, death, theatre, the gods, civilization triumphant over barbarism as image after image collapses, folding in on itself to form another: an Inca temple, the Pyramids, the Parthenon, the Colosseum, the Pantheon, Hagia Sophia, St.Mark's, Venice, St.Basil's, Moscow, Chartres, Salisbury, Amiens. Since the museum is closed to the public, only Henry and the pipe smoking men (redolent of an earlier era) are permitted to see the single, superficial images of these examples of Greek, Roman, Byzantine and Gothic architecture, now denuded of narrative context and understanding. It is a far cry from the celebration of the Dionysian spirit that prompted Henry's journey: if dreams are projections of our unconscious desires, then Richard consigns Henry to be a custodian of the lifeless relics of the past. As Richard watches Henry's receding back, he remains isolated and liminal, somewhere between a secret, private, subterranean ancient world and the modern world, which is in the process of being rebuilt, and where his status as outsider is confirmed. It is a fitting symbol for his narrative's end.

3

The Novel's Reception

The reception of *The Secret History* was divided in both Britain and the States. Opinions fluttered round the success or failure of characterisation, plot, genre, whether it was Brat-Pack, Southern Gothic, American Gothic or just American *Brideshead*. Reviewers noted that although the book's literary heritage derived from Euripides, Dostoevsky, Nietzsche, F. Scott Fitzgerald, Evelyn Waugh, T. S. Eliot, and Hitchcock's *Rope*, Tartt's achievement was only to be a Dostoevsky or Fitzgerald *manqué*, and was really borrowing the mantle of Bret Easton Ellis. Inevitably, an interest was registered in Tartt herself. Reviewers deliberated over whether *The Secret History* was or wasn't a 'whodunnit', a college coming-of-age story, a campus novel, a thriller, a novel about the nature of evil and so on. To some extent, book and author fell victim to predictions of its—and her—success as reviewers cavilled at the pre-publication hype and noted the tremendous advance, the sale of foreign rights and so on. So great was the demand for five-hundred page advance reader's editions of *The Secret History* that "Knopf had to print an unprecedented second run" noted James Kaplan in *Vanity Fair*.

Writing in *The Sunday Times*, Rebecca Mead was not alone in wondering whether a book could be over-hyped, and pointed out that even before most people had set eyes on *The Secret History*, several hundred thousand people now knew more about Donna Tartt than they ever really needed to: what she wore, where she bought her clothes and why, what brand cigarette she smoked now, what she smoked when she was seventeen and so on.[1] Needless to say, those involved in the promotion of Tartt denied that she was hyped: "They talk about Knopf's star-making machine," says Paul Bogards, Knopf's promotions co-ordinator. "We can't make stars . . ." a sentiment echoed almost verbatim by Tartt's creative writing tutor, Barry Hannah: "People call me a star-maker . . . Shit, Donna made herself." Tartt's own contemporaries echoed this view: Kaplan quotes Tartt's fellow Bennington student Jill Eisenstadt, "She was a sort of star early on. . . ." Knopf President Sonny Mehta is also "famous for his ability to catapult writers to stardom" and argued that there was an audience out there waiting to put her book in their briefcases and backpacks. Even Tartt's editor, Gary Fisketjohn added to the disavowals: "People say we're great at hyping, which I don't think is the case."

In the light of his comment, it's perhaps significant that both Jill Eisenstadt and Barry Hannah, insisting on Tartt's innate star quality, are cited in James Kaplan's *Vanity Fair* profile of Tartt, and it was this feature (or "breathless paean" as Ben McIntyre, reviewing for the London *Times* preferred) that unsettled some as a piece of shameless in-house promotion since Random House owns both *Vanity Fair* and Knopf, Tartt's American publishers. David Branyan, in the *National Review*, thought that "reasonable people" would be "sickened" by the *Vanity Fair* puff for Tartt and her novel, "which sets a new in-house record for delirious sycophancy." Much of McIntyre's criticism is reserved for the Random House publicity machine which was busy cranking up the volume of the ringing cash registers. This lament for literature as commodity fetish is underlined by Lee Lescaze's trenchant *Wall Street Journal* review, in which he is critical of both Random House and the novel: "Unfortunately publishers are more inclined to put their marketing dollars behind fiction like *The Secret History*, a work that amply demonstrates that a little learning is a tiresome thing." Pearl Bell, reviewing for *Partisan Review*, argued that the novel just couldn't justify its hype and failed to see what all the fuss had been about. Lescaze sided with her view: "As with much else these days, the hype causes the disappointment." So what was it about?

James Kaplan's *Vanity Fair* piece on Tartt dipped into her childhood and college years as it created a slightly freakish profile of her (she emerges as a curious amalgam of different fictive creations, from *Sunset Boulevard*'s Norma Desmond to "A Wise Child Out of Salinger"). In Kaplan's profile, *The Secret History* is that "hotly awaited highbrow chiller" which promises to be all things to all people: vastly entertaining *and* "extremely serious, and debatably "a book whose very essence is the survival of formality in a formality-starved era." Kaplan writes in high praise of Tartt's characterization, though he re-imagines (or fantasises?) her classicists as part of the English aristocratic landscape of fascist Mosley, the Mitfords, or the "bloody-toothed English schoolboys of *Lord of the Flies*."

In their "Anatomy of a Hype" review for *Newsweek*, Laura Shapiro and Ray Sawhill gave a rather more measured criticism of *The Secret History*, finding it "every inch a first novel" (whatever that means). Whereas Kaplan had contrived an imaginary socio-literary ancestry for Henry et al., Shapiro and Sawhill found the characters were "the weakest element" and found it impossible to distinguish between them without flipping back to Richard's initial descriptions of them (which perhaps speaks more to them as readers than to Tartt's depiction of her characters): "She adorns them with quirks," they observe, "but none has a personality . . ." They also found the novel amateurish and strained, as though she were "determined to Write a Novel, rather than eager to tell a story." James Wood also noted the punctiliousness of her plotting which threatened to stifle the vitality of her writing: "The story compels," he said, "but it doesn't involve."

In common with other reviewers, Pearl Bell in *Partisan Review* measured the novel against other generic types and found it wanting. For her this was a campus novel that failed as a detective story since we know who, how and why by the end of Book I. To compound its failure as detective story, Book II enacts the well-rehearsed dramas of the Brat-Pack drink, drugs and MTV generation: "Stupefied by a bottomless supply of valium, pot and cocaine, they mouth spurious, high-flown anguish that soon becomes unbearably boring." In fact, the Bennington or Brat Pack connection was frequently clutched at (though Tartt denied that Hampden was Bennington[2]), and as reviewers tried to place Tartt and her book, these connections formed a locus for assessing what kind of work she had inherited or developed. (The "Bennington Novel", Alexander Star wrote in the *New Republic*, is "a casually linked corpus of work produced by Bret Easton Ellis and Jill Eisenstadt in the mid-80s.") Some reviewers invoked the Brat Pack novel only to revoke it as a model by which Tartt's work might be assessed. Similarities (however superficial) between *The Rules of Attraction*, Ellis's second novel (set at "Camden"), and Tartt's novel (set at "Hampden") were always, nonetheless, going to be too conspicuous to ignore. Reviewers like Lescaze thought that Tartt's novel had far more in common with Ellis's writing than with the literary and classical tradition she also invokes in *The Secret History*. Shapiro and Sawhill, again, offered a more measured assessment, arguing that Ellis and Tartt are two very different writers, even though their Yuppified characters seem to hail from the same stock.

Yet although reviewers of her novel saw parallels with the Brat-Pack commentaries on the sybaritic youth of 1980s America, they were also divided as to whether her novel was, as McIntyre believed, distinct and different, or whether Tartt was delivering more of the same formulaic stuff, as Nancy Wood inferred: "With its cast of young, hedonistic characters and its collegiate setting, *The Secret History* could well have been written using the *Spy* Novel-O-Matic."[3] So long as *The Secret History* was locked into this literary model, praise or condemnation for it rested on whatever you thought about the Brat Pack *oeuvre*. But again, the reviews offer little consensus. What distinguished her novel from the Brat-Pack was her talent, with Tartt's value notable principally because of the perceived intellectual paucity of the times. Ben McIntyre in the *Times* celebrated the fact that here was a novelist under 30 who read more books than she did magazines, and suggested that this was what distinguished her from her 1980s predecessors. For while Tartt "peeled back the mottled skin of youth culture", she also communicated a familiarity with Nabokov, Buddha, Nietzsche, Pound, Eliot, Poe, Salinger and Plato. While others paid similar accolades in support of Tartt's learning (James Kaplan had also observed that "She quotes freely and naturally from Thomas Aquinas, Cardinal Newman, Buddha, and Plato — as well as David Byrne of *Talking Heads* and Jonathon Richman of the *Modern Lovers*. And many others."), others dismissed her knowledge as no more than name-dropping, a little learning, as Lescaze cautioned, being a tiresome thing.

In her *Partisan Review* notice, Pearl Bell thought that the novel had only "pretensions to erudition and moral seriousness." Again, Lescaze shared her reservations: "*The Secret History* may prove to be a best seller . . . but it is not literary." Indeed, he argued that its literariness was nothing more than a pose (a criticism also leveled against her characterization, described variously as cardboard, not entirely plausible, with characters indistinguishable from each other, or as "stand-up targets"[4] or as having "no life outside their poses."[5]) The distinction between Tartt's novel and other Brat Pack novels, then, lies only in the fact that she dips into the Western Literary Canon, rather than popular culture: the allusions, suggests Andrew Rosenheim in the *New York Times*, are superficial. Yet the references and allusions that she makes are too many to be summarily dismissed.

Amanda Vaill in *The Washington Post* was kinder to the novel, noting the literary and classical references in the book's acknowledgements: Paul McGloin was her "muse and Maecenas", who, Vaill notes, was the patron of Horace and Virgil. Tartt borrows T. S. Eliot's dedication of *The Wasteland* to Pound when she acknowledges her editor, Gary Fisketjohn *"il miglior fabbro"* (the better craftsman). That Vaill found this "pretty heady stuff" is either testimony to Lescaze's caution about a little learning (what, after all, *is* heady about the allusions?), or else her comments resonate with McIntyre's praise of Tartt's range of reference. But Vaill's catalog of references always take us back to T. S. Eliot. Many reviewers noted that Tartt's use of Bunny as a nickname for Edmund Corcoran chimes with critic and writer Edmund Wilson's nickname, but when Vaill pushes the point, she gets to Wilson's *Axel's Castle* which contains an essay on Eliot. Similarly, Hampden's French professor, Georges Laforgue, is possibly named after Jules Laforgue, the French symbolist poet and an early influence for Eliot.

Indeed, in his *Vanity Fair* profile of Tartt, James Kaplan suggested that "As good a place to begin as any is the fact that she has a largish obsession, bordering on the cultic, with T. S. Eliot." He also noted the "thicket of literary references and inside jokes" in the novel, although when he pointed out to her that the Albermarle Hotel named in her novel was also the name of the hotel that Eliot recuperated in after a breakdown, she became "chilly" and told him "I have nothing to say about that." In determining what *we* might have to say to that (since presumably there *is* something to say about it), Vaill suggests that Tartt is attempting to write herself into a literary tradition "that extends from classical to modern literature." But in her self-conscious attention to such allusions, Vaill wondered whether or not Tartt would in the end make a merely interesting writer rather than a truly great one. Interestingly, while comparisons with Eliot and Fitzgerald (added to Kaplan's imagined 1930s English heritage for the characters) suggest a relationship with Anglo-American literary modernism, other readings of the novel have observed a closer relationship to the Victorians.

Tartt's "fleshy, well-formed sentences"[6] contrast sharply with the postmodern fractured surface of Ellis's prose style. Ben McIntyre in the London *Times* also found the allusions, depth and texture of Tartt's prose style to "owe much more to the 19th century than to the 20th." James Wood, reviewing in the *London Review of Books* endorsed the pleasures of Tartt's prose style, a pleasure made all the more profound because "it is startling to find it so openly done in a contemporary American novel." Her fiction reminded him of Swift and Dickens, because she had, he said, returned a sense of wonderment to fiction.

Vaill praises (*contra* reviewers like Bell) Tartt's ability to craft a suspenseful plot, particularly in the aftermath of Bunny's funeral. She also praised Tartt's talent as a writer, singling out scenes such as Henry absent-mindedly smearing earth over his shirt at Bunny's funeral. Also writing in praise of Tartt's mastery of narrative suspense was Andrew Rosenheim in the *New York Times* (Book Review). Although he found moments of "irritating pretension" (where others have noted Tartt's "closed and rarefied world [created] with affectionate precision"[7]), he also praised Tartt's novel for being "a gripping read" and for her "rich descriptive style" or again, "its many magnificent pages of description . . ." (Other reviewers, such as Bell and Duffy, have praised her powers of description, attributing this to her being a southern writer, or have seen the novel in terms of a southern gothic tradition.) But what gripped some bored others, and although John Sutherland recognized the narrative's desire to be hypnotic, he found it instead narcotic and wished she had shown her manuscript to a "ruthless editor as well as to her indulgent college friend." Alexander Star wrote in approval of Tartt's handling of her narrative, particularly in Book II as members of the group begin to disintegrate: "It is the accumulation of these troubles, narrated with detached foreboding, that gives the book its slow creeping force."

And while there was much criticism levelled at Tartt's narrator in terms of characterization and (for Lescaze) as a device to mask her own limited powers of description, Star and Wood both found Richard a clever and sometimes compelling invention, since narrator and reader become identified, particularly at moments of suspense in the novel: Star isolates Julian's slow discovery of Bunny's revelatory letter as one of those suspenseful scenes which "slyly parodies its own page-turning momentum." Wood chooses a moment from earlier in the narrative when Richard first seeks Julian out, and as his face first peers out at Richard, ". . . the narrator becomes the reader, and we share an ecstasy of wide-eyedness." It kept Wood happy, anyway, and he pronounced the novel "a prolonged and happy 'Geez'." Slightly less happy was John Sutherland, who in the *Times Literary Supplement* thought that Richard was "a Gatsbyish narrator, who admits to having a mediocre mind and displays it by his every turn of phrase, never quite understanding what he chronicles."

Rosenheim is among the reviewers who found aspects of the plot less than convincing, although later and longer critical essays (such as Barbara Melvin's) have argued that some of the initial reviewers of the book were guilty of showing a bias against classics, and Francois Pauw's careful analysis explains much of the Classical subtext in the novel. Bias against the classics is evident in reviews like that of Nancy Wood in *Macleans* who found the classicists self-indulgent and pretentious when they "enter into obscure discussions about Greek philosophers and poets." Hence the murder of the farmer during the bacchanal is less convincing than the murder of Bunny which is provoked by "baser motives" (fear of capital punishment or life imprisonment). Again, critical arguments like Barbara Melvin's in the *Journal of Evolutionary Psychology* (March 1992), suggest that such a reading of the novel is to trivialize or disregard Tartt's appeal to a classical tradition. James Wood is among this group in finding the classicists' implausibility a novelistic strategy, which would protect them from "the censure of realism." Kaplan, on the other hand, paid a predictably handsome tribute to Tartt's "ability to make us believe, utterly, in all this — at the moment of sacred insanity, we are one with the celebrants. We would follow her tumbling, mellifluous prose anywhere." A less handsome but much sweeter compliment came from an infatuated James Wood who found the novel "swoonily compulsive."

How might we account for such differences in the reception of the novel? Clearly, the novel stands or falls according to where the reviewer wants to locate it which proves to be anywhere in the literary tradition stretching back to Plato and Euripides and borrowing from the European and American nineteenth and twentieth century traditions, as well as the more recent 'Brat Pack' 1980s novelists. There's much to be engaged with and to feel frustrated at here — and the same goes for the novel's far from straightforward relationship to literary genres with which it has some sport.

Some consensus is apparent in the respective readings of Andrew Rosenheim's *New York Times* Book Review and Barbara Melvin's essay. Rosenheim applauds Tartt's "skillful investigation of the chasm between academe's supposed ideals and the vagaries of its actual behaviour." This investigation returns us to the theme of reality and illusion, which Tartt readily admitted was one of the "themes" of her book. But reality and illusion form only one of the many binary pairings that structure the novel. *The Secret History* straddled the perceived divisions between commercial and critical success. It was and it wasn't a Bennington novel. Tartt had an ear for realism, best evinced in her rendition of the vernacular of Judy Poovey or Cloke Rayburn. Wood suggested that Tartt was torn between her classicists and the MTV generation, and that that division was readable in terms of thinking that the novel supplies the reader's wants, as well as her own: ". . . just as the novel too happily satisfies the reader's wants, so, perhaps, these unlikely Classics students satisfy her own wants?"

Suggestions have been made as to why Tartt's novel experienced these mixed reviews. Barbara Melvin, in an essay written four years after publication of *The Secret History* has suggested that "There are two facets to *The Secret History* centering on classical issues which simultaneously make the work powerful and yet have contributed negatively to its critical reception. These are the author's use of classical ideas and her contrast with modern American morality."[8] Melvin suggests, though this can only be speculative, that there's a perception of classics as being politically incorrect (though no review really substantiates such a notion) or that there's resentment at Tartt's knowledge of the classics.

John Sutherland's bemusement by Julian Morrow's selectively chosen small groups and the fact that the students take no other classes with any other teacher is, for Melvin, to ignore the precedent or 'classical echo' as she has it: "The idea of one teacher is unthinkable in academia today, but in classical Greece was the norm. As Julian himself points out, Plato had only Socrates, Aristotle only Plato, and Alexander the Great, only Aristotle to teach him." As Melvin says, "It is an indication of Julian's exalted opinion of himself that he matter-of-factly includes himself in this list", but this too echoes some reviewers' thoughts about Tartt's literary allusiveness and uses of intertextuality in her novel, as though to locate herself within the Western canon: whether this locates her more as a reader of the Western canon than as a participant in it is clearly a matter for debate.

4

The Novel's Performance

Ellis introduced Tartt to his own agent, Amanda "Binky" Urban who reportedly said "My god, it's incredibly well-written—I couldn't stop turning the pages." (*Vanity Fair*) Urban started competitive bidding for the book in the Spring of 1991, prior to the annual American Booksellers Association convention. Knopf triumphed, to the reputed sum of $450,000.

It's been suggested that Donna Tartt was simply in the right place at the right time:

"The book might not have caused such a fuss if it had been bought at another time of year," says an editor at another [publishing] house. Knopf kept the buzz going all year by sending galleys to booksellers, whipping up the sales force to pitch the book and using the 1992 A[nnual] B[ooksellers] A[ssociation] to hawk the novel and introduce Tartt to booksellers and reviewers.[1]

Even Tartt herself has commented on what she perceived to be a "piece of cataclysmic luck." ["Anatomy of a Hype"] as she acknowledged that "[t]here are plenty of extraordinary people who write books far better than this and don't get half this attention." ["Anatomy of a Hype"] Along with the $450,000 advance came a further $500,000 from sales of foreign rights to 11 different countries (including France, Germany, Italy, Holland, Norway, Sweden, Finland, Spain, Portugal and Greece). At 75,000, the first print run was 65,000 more than was usual for first novels. Tartt went on a 20-city publicity tour, her book entered the *New York Times* bestseller lists at number 10, and remained in the list for 13 weeks. In 1993, *The Secret History* went on to win the Dutch and Flemish Mekka Prize.

Movie rights were sold to the distinguished director, producer and screenwriter Alan J. Pakula (*All the President's Men*; *The Pelican Brief*; *Presumed Innocent*). They are currently with Scott Hicks, director of *Shine* and *Snow Falling on Cedars*. As Tartt herself has said, "It's been up and down and around and through."[2] Back in 1997 it still wasn't in production and as far as she knew then, script writers (Rafael Yglesias has been named) were still working on it. Although she's said that she tried to keep up with where it was at the beginning, she began to lose interest "after about five years" (which would actually take her to 1997, the time of the interview). As with her second novel, at time of going to press, we're still waiting for news.

There's been much speculation amongst *The Secret History aficionados* who, in the absence of the big screen version have imagined who might play who (Ethan Hawke as Richard, Jude Law as Francis, Chloe Sevigny as Camilla, Matt Damon as Bunny, or a young Charles Laughton as Bunny, a young James Mason or Richard Burton for Henry), even down to what soundtrack would be fitting. Interestingly, there's also some reluctance to see this visually suggestive text adapted for screen, a reluctance which is in part a tribute to Tartt's powers as a writer.

It's difficult to assess whether or not Tartt began a trend, continued one or actually ended one. Alexander Star, writing in the *New*

Republic, noted that ". . . the Bennington novel may be entering a new phase, or at least Donna Tartt . . . has written something different."[3] In other words, *The Secret History* both was and wasn't a Bennington novel; similar enough to the Brat Pack to see them as possible predecessors, but also different enough to unsettle the expectations aroused by works like Ellis's *Less Than Zero, The Rules of Attraction* or even Jay McInerney's *Bright Lights, Big City*. Although James Wood thought that Tartt seemed torn between wanting to give readers more of the same (like the frolics of the MTV-generation) he also recognized that the novel's distinction and achievement lay in its literary allusions and ambitions. In other words, Tartt borrows from something immediately recognizable but develops the campus novels in a different direction. Although she satirizes a particular way of life, it's only an aspect of her novel, not its defining characteristic.

And has it spawned imitators? Not quite, but once reviewers and critics begin to judge novels subsequent to *The Secret History* in relation to it, then a distinctive recognizable sub-genre will emerge. Indeed, reviewers have cited *The Secret History* as a touchstone in assessing Richard Mason's *The Drowning People* (1999), a labored murder mystery which strains to "write well" and renders *The Secret History* a masterpiece by comparison. It's a retrospectively told narrative in which secret histories are finally revealed, its structure and ambitions don't really bear that much scrutiny and actually, any comparison limits Tartt's novel to being not much more than a murder mystery.

5

Further Reading

Donna Tartt

The Secret History New York: Alfred A. Knopf 1992

Short Stories

*"Tam O'Shanter", *The New Yorker*, April 1993.
*"A Christmas Pageant," *Harpers* 287.1723, December, 1993.
"A Garter Snake," GQ 65:5, May, 1995
*"True Crime" in *Murder for Love, Murder for Women*, Dove Audio, 1996.

Non-fiction

*"Sleepytown: A Southern Gothic Childhood, with Codeine," *Harper's* 286, July, 1992. 60–66
"Basketball Season" in *The Best American Sports Writing*, Frank Deford (ed.), Houghton Mifflin: 1993.
*"Team Spirit: Memories of Being a Freshman Cheerleader for the Basketball Team", *Harper's* 288, April, 1994: 37–40.

"The Spirit and Writing in a Secular World", pp. 25–40 in Fiddes Paul (ed.), *The Novel: Spirituality and Modern Culture: Eight Novelists Write About Their Craft and Context*. Cardiff: University of Wales Press, 2000.

*Available at "The Unofficial Donna Tartt *Secret History* Site"

Features by Donna Tartt in the Oxford American

'Spirituality in the Modern Novel,' *Oxford American* issue #30, Nov/Dec 1999.

"Willie Morris 1934–1999," *Oxford American* Issue #29, Sept/Oct 1999.

"The Belle and the Lady," *Oxford American* Issue #26, March-May.

"Murder and Imagination: Further Reflections on a Fine Art," *Oxford American*.

Special Double Issue on Crime, Spring 1996.

"In Melbourne," *Oxford American*, March/April 1995.

"True Crime" (poem), *Oxford American* Issue #4, 1993/4.

"Basketball Season," *Oxford American* Issue #2, 1992.

(Back issues of *The Oxford American* are available through their website: *www.oxfordamericanmag.com*)

Web Sites

Many of these web sites cross reference each other, so you're as likely to come across them that way. Individual addresses are as follows:

http://www.olemiss.edu/depts/english/ms-writers/dir/tartt_donna/ You'll find links to Barry Hannah and Willie Morris here, as well as on-line reviews of *The Secret History*, a list of publications and adaptations, a bibliography and a guide to other internet resources which will take you to:

http://www.geocities.com/SoHo/8543/dmain.htm — The Unofficial Donna Tartt/Secret History Web Page, hosted by Alex, is a good, informative and informal place. Alex's page contains a useful bibliography of works by and about Tartt, as well as a chat room, a transcript of a radio interview hosted by Ray Suarez with Donna Tartt and Ann Rice "Halloween: Gothic Literature. A conversation with Anne Rice and Donna

Tartt on National Public Radio's "Talk of the Nation", October 30th 1997. There's pretty up-to-date information about her second novel and also the rumored film production, and contact details for Tartt's agent, Amanda Urban, and Knopf, her American publishers. You'll also find the asterixed essays (noted above) on this site. The site will also link you to:

http://www.btinternet.com/~buckleburyweb/sh.htm- a review of *The Secret History* by Adrian McOram Cambell. The page contains other links which will take you back The Mississippi Writers Page (olemiss.edu) as well as to *The Unofficial Donna Tartt/Secret History Web Page.* This site will also take you to a Mythography site, Exploring Greek, Roman and Celtic Mythology and Art. You can also access a couple of other book reviews:

http://www.dannyreviews.com/h/The_Secret_History.html
See also:

http://clubs.yahoo.com/clubs/the secret history — run by Idomoneus and worth a visit. The quality of the chats vary between discussions about characterization, imagining who would play which character in a film, and those of classical scholars with a more specialist (though no less enthusiastic) understanding. But there are some interesting speculations on the time scale of the events in the novel, discussions about characterisation as well as the classical and literary intertexts of *The Secret History*, along with a discussion about the significance of the etymological root of 'fern', and what exactly the films are that Richard is dispatched to see on the night of the murder. There are some real aficionados out there.

You can also access or contact directly a short review article on TSH, "We Other Dionysians: Devolving the Marginal Elite in Tartt's *The Secret History*" at *http://www.womenwriters.net/archives/bartlett1199.htm*

Newspaper and Magazine Reviews

Allen, Brooke. "Panpipes and Preppies," *The New Criterion.* 11:2 October 1992, pp. 65–8.

Bell, Pearl K. *Partisan Review,* 60: (1), pp. 63–5. Winter 1993, pp. 63–5.

Branyan, David. *National Review* 44:69. 5 October 1992.

Duffy, Martha. "Murder Midst the Ferns." *Time* 140.9 31, August 1992, p. 69.

Fosburgh, Lacey. "Forbidden and Gothic." *Vogue* 182, September 1992, p. 380.

Hajari, Nisid. Review of *The Secret History* VLS 108, September 1992, p. 7.

*Kaplan, James. "Smartt Tartt." *Vanity Fair* 55:9, September 1992, ⟵ pp. 248–51.

Krist, Gary. *The Secret History Hudson Review* 46: (1), Spring 1993, pp. 239–46.

Lescaze, Lee. "Groves of Academe Shed Gold and Yawns." *Wall Street Journal*, 9 Sept 1992, A12.

McIntyre, Ben. "Tartt Bites the Big Apple." "Life and Times." p. 5 in *The Times*, September 2 1992.

Mead, Rebecca. "Smart Tartt." p. 8, Section 8, *Sunday Times*. September 27 1992.

Rosenheim, Andrew. "Dead Guy on Campus." *The New York Times* (Book Review), Sept 13 1992, p. 3.

Saynor, James. "The Wrong Stuff." *The Observer*, 25 October 1992, p. 65.

Star, Alexander. "Less Than Hero." *New Republic* 4,057, Oct 19th 1992, pp. 47–49.

Sutherland, John. *Times Literary Supplement* 4673, p. 20, Oct 23rd 1992.

Vail, Amanda. "Beyond Good and Evil." Book World *The Washington Post* 13, September 1992, p. 3, 9.

Wood, James. "The Glamour of Glamour." *London Review of Books* 14:22, 19 November 1992, pp. 17–18.

Wood Nancy. "A Lethal Frenzy: Pagan Rites Go Wrong in a Compelling Novel." *Maclean's*, 12 October 1992, p. 85, Vol 105: 41.

*Also available on The Unofficial Secret History site.

Journal Articles: *The Secret History*

Arkins, Brian. "Greek Themes in Donna Tartt's *The Secret History. Classical and Modern Literature: A Quarterly*, Spring 1995, 15:3, pp. 281–87.

Eisenstadt, Jill. Interview BOMB. Fall 1992, 41, pp. 56–9.

Melvin, Barbara. "Failures in Classical and Modern Morality: Echoes of Euripides in *The Secret History. Journal of Evolutionary Psychology*, March 1996, 17: 1–2, pp. 53–63.

*Pauw, Francois. "If on a Winter's Night a Reveller: The Classical Intertext in Donna Tartt's *The Secret History. Akroterion*, 39:3 / 4, 1994, pp. 141–163.

*Pauw, Francois. "If on a Winter's Night a Reveller: The Classical Intertext in Donna Tartt's *The Secret History. Akroterion*, 40:1, 1995, pp. 2–29.

*These are the most comprehensive journal articles available on *The Secret History*, commenting in detail on the classical intertext in the novel.

Journal Articles referring to *The Secret History*

Boyd, E. "Sister Act: Sorority Rush as Feminine Performance (American South)." *Southern Cultures*, 5: (3) 54–73, Fall 1999.

Caenpeel, M. "Aspect and Text Structure." *Linguistics*, 33: (2), pp. 213–253, 1995.

Ober, J. "Responsible Popularization Classics: An Introduction." *Classical Bulletin*, 75: (2), pp. 85–91 1996.

Ruprecht L. A. "Whither the Neo-Hellenic? Hellenism on Display." *Journal of Modern Greek Studies*, 15: (2), pp. 247–260, Oct 1997.

Ward, G. "Transcorporeality: The Ontological Scandal (The Body Physical as Transfigured Through Christian Theology)." *Bulletin of the John Rylands University Library*, Manchester 80: (3), pp. 235–252, Fall 1998.

Suggested further reading

Dante Alighieri. *The Comedy of Dante Alighieri Cantica 1 Hell (L'Inferno)*. Trans. Dorothy L. Sayers, Harmondsworth: Penguin, 1949.

Dickens, Charles. *Our Mutual Friend*. Harmondsworth: Penguin, 1997.

Dodds, E. R. "The Blessings of Madness." pp. 64–101 in *The Greeks and the Irrational*, California: California University Press, 1951.

Dostoevsky, Fyodor. *Crime and Punishment* (1865–6). Harmondsworth: Penguin, 1988.

Eliot, T. S. *Collected Poems*. London: Faber and Faber, 1963.

Eliot, T. S. *Collected Essays*. London: Faber and Faber 1951.

Ellis, Bret Easton. *Less Than Zero*. London: Picador 1986.

Ellis, Bret Easton. *The Rules of Attraction*. London: Picador 1988.

Ellis, Bret Easton. *American Psycho*. London: Picador 1991.

Euripides. *Bacchae and Other Plays*. Trans. James Morwood, Intro, Edith Hall Oxford: OUP 1999.

Fitzgerald, F Scott. *The Great Gatsby*. (1926) Introduction, Tony Tanner. Harmondsworth: Penguin 1990.

Fowles, John. *The Magus*. Hertfordshire: Triad/Granada, 1978.

Marlowe, Christopher. *Doctor Faustus* (A- and B- texts 1604, 1616). Eds. David Bevington, Eric Rasmussen. Manchester: Manchester University Press, 1993.

Nietzsche, Friedrich. *The Birth of Tragedy*. Trans Douglas Smith. Oxford: OUP, 1997.

Nietzsche, Friedrich. *Beyond Good and Evil*. Trans. Walter Kaufman, New York: Vintage Books, 1989.

Paglia, Camille. "Apollo and Dionysus." pp. 72–98 in *Sexual Personae: Art and Decadence from Nefertiti to Emily Dickinson*. London & New Haven: Yale University Press, 1990.

Petronius, trans. P. G. Walsh. *The Satyricon*. Oxford: OUP, 1997.

Plato *Republic*. Trans. Robin Waterfield. Oxford: OUP, 1993.

Waugh, Evelyn. *Brideshead Revisited*. Harmondsworth: Penguin 1981.

Wilson, Edmund. "T. S.Eliot." pp. 93–131 in *Axel's Castle: A Study in the Imaginative Literature of 1870–1930*. New York: Charles Scribner's Sons, 1959.

Related reading: texts alluded or referred to in *The Secret History*

As many readers of *The Secret History* have noted, there are a raft of allusions to other classical and literary sources in it, as well as a list of popular texts and films. In order of appearance, these are:

Epigraph, Book I: Nietzsche *Unzeitgemasse Betrachtungen (Untimely Meditations)*; Plato *The Republic* Book II. As a child, Richard recalls reading *Tom Swift* (the popular counterparts to *Tom Swift*, the *Rover Boys* and the *Bobbsey Twins* series, are located at Francis's grandmother's house) and Tolkien (p. 8). As an adolescent, and prior to his arrival at Hampden, he reads Milton (p. 10) and Pythagoras (p. 11). At Hampden, when he first attends Julian's Greek classes, Julian tells him not to buy Roth's *Goodbye, Columbus* (p. 30); Richard alludes to Aristotle's *Poetics* (p. 36), *The Orestia* (p. 36), *The Iliad* (p. 37), the *Bacchae* (p. 38), and Plato's dialogue, *Parmenides*. Bunny and Henry are described by Charles and Camilla as "L'Allegro" and "Il Penseroso," both poems by John Milton (p. 59) Richard also notes that his favorite novel is *The Great Gatsby* (p. 68).

At Francis's grandmother's house, a more eclectic cultural mix is evident: the impression is that she's a bibliophile, and irrespective of the cultural value or importance of the books there, they're now valuable as commodities or collectibles. On her bookshelves, Richard discovers a first edition of *Ivanhoe*; the enormously popular Victorian writer Marie Corelli, old copies of the *Rover Boys*, and the *Bobbsey Twins* — if, as seems probable, these are first editions, they're all highly collectible. Also there are Thomas Pennant's *London* (date not given, but a first edition would be 1790), *The Club History of London*, the libretto for *The Pirates of Penzance* and an 1821 edition (which would make it an enormously valuable first edition) of Byron's *Marino Falerio*.

Part III of *The Wasteland*, "The Fire Sermon" is quoted when Richard recollects a boating scene at the house. At this house, too, Henry translates Milton from English to Latin, Bunny reads (and hides from Julian) *The Bride of Fu Manchu*, (now racist and ludicrously sexist to modern sensibilities, but a comment perhaps on Bunny's xenophobic and misogynistic tendencies, as well as the sinister machinations of a zvengali who manipulates innocent victims). Francis reads the *Memoirs of the Duc de St Simon* (p. 89) and reference is specifically made to Dorothy Sayers' translation of the *Divine Comedy (Inferno))*, p. 157. (Sayers's translation of *Inferno* is also what Bunny takes with him on his trip to Italy with Henry, p. 99 although he presumably doesn't need it in order to transform the Piazza di Spagna "into a simulacrum of Hell." That it's Dorothy L Sayers's edition again gestures towards the criminal/detective status of the novel.) Charles teaches Richard to play piquet "because it's what Rawdon Crawley plays in *Vanity Fair*" (p. 94) After their return to Hampden for the new semester, Richard tries to fend off his growing sense of unease at the rest of the group's mysterious behaviour by reading Raymond Chandler. (p. 131)

Reference is also made to Hitchcock's film version of John Buchan's *The Thirty Nine Steps* (Richard and Bunny go to see it on the night of the Bacchanal, p. 168). The text's status as detective/crime fiction is underlined when Francis compares them all, post-bacchanal to being "—all white robes and bloody like something from Edgar Allan Poe." (p. 169) Reference is also made to what Homer says about the Arcadians in the *Iliad* (p. 196) and to Plato's definition of Justice in *The Republic* where everyone's happy within their own place in the social hierarchy (p. 199). Henry picks up Dante's *Purgatorio* while he's discussing the possibilities of poisoning Bunny (p. 220), an idea which is then dismissed as being "so Walter Scott" (p. 235). Other film references are to *The Wizard of Oz* (before Bunny is killed, Richard feels this is what Kansas must have been like before the cyclone hit, and later, when Julian discovers that Henry murdered Bunny, Richard describes the theatrical curtain falling away to reveal a much more ordinary Julian).

Book II begins with another epigraph, from ER Dodds's *The Greeks and the Irrational*, underlining the novel's exploration of Dionysian chaos. References scattered throughout Book II are to: *The Aeneid*; the *Upanishads*, which Henry reads during his stay at the Corcorans for Bunny's funeral. This resonates with Part V, "What the Thunder Said" in *The Wasteland*: *The Upanishads* are cited twice in lines 401 and 433; AE Housman, whose poem, "With rue my heart is laden" Henry reads at the funeral. Richard wonders why he didn't read from the *Upanishads* or from Milton's *Lycidas*. Dostoevsky is alluded to (Raskolnikov's admission of murder is quoted from *Crime and Punishment*) as well as *Phaedo*; Francis reveals that as a child undergoing psychotherapy, he identified with Davy in *Kidnapped*: Davy, in constant pursuit across the Scottish highlands is not unlike Richard Hannay in *The Thirty-Nine Steps*); Richard takes PG Wodehouse to Charles in hospital (p. 447) and Henry reminds him of a crazed gardener in *Alice in Wonderland* (p. 461); Charles resembles the old pirate in *Treasure Island* during his last stay at Francis's house. Richard also reads *The Malcontent* (he describes himself as a "brooding malcontent" early in his narrative); *The White Devil; The Broken Heart* (cited in the epigraph to the Epilogue); *The Revenger's Tragedy; Doctor Faustus* (whose rejection of learning and damnation serves as a cautionary tale rather too late for Richard or, indeed, Henry); and *Our Mutual Friend* which, like *Crime and Punishment* and like *The Secret History*, explores the psychology of a crime.

Other works by Donna Tartt

"Tam-O'-Shanter" (*The New Yorker*, April 1993) is a short story about an old actor called Geordie McTavish (real name Gordon Burns), a child actor who had been an extra in a 1936 film version of *Our Mutual Friend*, with Joan Fontaine, Laurence Olivier and Alec Guiness. (There is no such film, though the book also makes a brief appearance at the end of *The Secret History*.) Now an elderly man with cancer, Gordon/Geordie visits small children who are ill or dying in hospital, and has to countenance their disappointment every time, when, secure in their belief in the immortality conferred by the big screen, they confront the old man that the screen child inevitably became. The story stalks questions of identity, mortality and immortality, illusion and reality, ending with Gordon/Geordie visiting a sick little girl who seems stuck between very old age and a fragile infancy. At the moment he enters the room, it's as though he re-enters his own childhood, and the little girl welcomes him with a wisdom apparently far beyond her years. As she does so, Gordon willingly, happily, becomes the professionally Scottish "Geordie" of his Hollywood Studio years.

"A Christmas Pageant" (*Harpers*, 1993) uses a narrative voice sympathetic to the point of view of another wise child, a pious, precocious little girl called Sally, a fourth grader who both feels that she is different, and is made to feel different, to all the other little girls. The narrative focuses on the school's Christmas Pageant, where nine of the children rehearse a short rhyme to accompany the single letter they wear and which, collectively, will spell CHRISTMAS. To Sally's disgust, the spirituality of Christmas has been denuded for the sake of its social trimmings. Consequently, C is not for Christ but for Candy, H is not for Herod but for Holly and so on.

Backstage, the adults' social banter focuses on the need to appropriately observe social roles. Thus, Sally's mother is found wanting because she's not at the Pageant which makes Sally want to defend her against the spiteful comments of the other mothers and teachers. Set against the relatively affluent but occasionally motherless Sally is the poor, dirty, "trailer trash" Kenny Priddy. As the Pageant unfolds in all its stale predictability, Kenny's criminal father suddenly bursts into the venue, holds a knife against Kenny's mother's throat, and demands access to his son, and the tame, polite Christmas Pageant becomes desperate and savage. And so the story of Christmas is transformed; no longer about the birth of Jesus but a poignant event, seen by Sally as a raw display of paternal longing, and perceived by the others as a violent threat to personal safety, where the criminal edge of America intrudes upon the complaisant small town. But the point of the story shifts emphasis continuously. As parents and children clear the stage, a child called Tammy, and Kenny and Sally remain there. And of the three, Sally is the one not wanted, feared for or apparently cared for. Mr Priddy (Henry Lee) lets Mrs Priddy (RaeLynn) go when he shifts his anger to Tammy's mother for setting her dog on him and giving him a bruise the size of a grapefruit. This relatively comic denouement ends with the police successfully re-capturing Henry Lee. Sally, unnoticed throughout, calls for one of the servants at home to come and pick her up. Sitting quietly and alone as she waits for him, she hears one of the teacher's inserting herself into the drama as she lies to the police about being held at knife point. For Sally, a miracle has occurred, and still no one has believed, and it is tempting to speculate, with *The Secret History* in mind, that the miracle is Henry Lee Priddy's overpowering desire, at the cost of his liberty, to see his son again, that fathers really do love their children.

The intrusion of the violent into the anodyne features in "True Crime", a poem submitted to a collection of stories called *Murder for Love* (Delta, 1996), and in which she sutures a relation between criminality and desire. The authorial voice in the poem observes, but never enters, the deluded mind of a cannibalistic murderer who exists in a perverse and private realm where norms and taboos collide in a series of understatements ("I have a problem. I'm/A Cannibal"). Small town violence and myth (he's at his worst during a full moon) co-operate in the scenario, then, to undo strict

\etween fiction and fact. Full moons which prompt diabolical
‌   may be the stuff of gothic fancy, but Tartt's villain (or at least,
‌   wno report his story) have ingested this as fact. The poem places his
modest aspirations (he thinks of operating a candy business part-time) side
by side with his murderous desires, symbolised by his crude stick figure
drawings of a childhood love on the barrel of his gun, all of which speaks
to, in Hannah Arendt's phrase, the banality of evil.

Discussion Questions

1. Did the group have to be Classicists? Would a different story have
   emerged if they'd studied something different? How integral is Classics
   to the novel, or to your reading of the novel?
2. To what extent is Julian culpable for the events of the novel? Or, indeed,
   how credibly realized is his character?
3. Does the novel suffer for having a first-person narrator? Does this limit
   characterization, perspective, point of view?
4. Reviewers found Tartt's characters one dimensional: to what extent do
   you think they *are* assembled only by their recognizable wardrobes and
   phrases?
5. Why is Bunny in the group at all, given that he has no aptitude whatso-
   ever for the subject?
6. The novel has been described as a seduction into evil: where does the
   seduction start, and who or what is evil?
7. How could Bunny have been involved with the rest of the group for
   months if they'd only decided to perform the Bacchanal after Richard
   joins the group? (Henry reminds Richard about the seminar, and says
   that that's when they first thought of it. Is he telling the truth?)
8. "I am sorry, as well, to present such a sketchy and disappointing exegesis
   of what is in fact the central part of my story." TSH, p. 261 What *is* the
   central part of Richard's story?
9. Why does Bunny suggest to Richard that he joins their group? And why
   does Julian accept him?
10. What *is* the meaning of Richard's final dream?

Notes

1. Donna Tartt: Biography and Influences

1. "Sleepytown: A Southern Gothic Childhood with Codeine."

2. James Kaplan, *Vanity Fair*

3. "Talking with Donna Tartt—Cinderella Story" Interview with Pam Lambert, reproduced from *Newsday* 4th October 1992 p. 34 This interview is available on *http://www.geocities.com/SoHo/8543/dmain.htm* at *The Unofficial Donna Tartt/Secret History* website.

4. "The Spirit and Writing in a Secular World" p. 33

5. Interview available on *The Unofficial Donna Tartt/ Secret History* Web Page.

6. Taken from a profile of Donna Tartt in the *New York Times* Book Review

7. "Wish You Were Here: Oxford, Mississippi", *Elle Magazine* October 94

8. "The Spirit and Writing in a Secular World" p. 33

9. Interview with Pam Lambert *The Unofficial Donna Tartt/Secret History* Web Page

10. See "The Spirit and Writing in a Secular World" pp. 25–40

11. "The Spirit and Writing in a Secular World" p. 38

Notes

2. Reading *The Secret History*

1. All page references to the novel are taken from the Viking (Penguin Group) 1992 edition. To help locate references for different editions, Chapter 1: pp. 8–43; Chapter 2: pp. 44–97; Chapter 3: pp. 98–128; Chapter 4: pp. 129–162; Chapter 5 pp. 163–254; Chapter 6: pp. 259–353; Chapter 7: 354–395; Chapter 8:pp. 396–504; Epilogue: pp. 509–524

2. "The Spirit and Writing in a Secular World" p. 37

3. Camille Paglia, *Sexual Personae* pp. 102–3

4. François Pauw, "If on a Winter's Night a Reveller: The Classical Intertext in Donna Tartt's *The Secret History Akroterion* I, p. 143

5. Adrian Poole, Introduction, *Our Mutual Friend*, p. x

6. "The Spirit and Writing in a Secular World" p. 38

7. Martin Swales *The Art of Detective Fiction* London: Macmillan 2000

8. Patrick ffrench, "Open Letter to Detectives and Psychoanalysts: Analysis and Reading" p. 225 in *The Art of Detective Fiction*

9. Douglas Smith, Introduction, *The Birth of Tragedy* p. xx

10. *The Birth of Tragedy*, p. xx

11. Bram Rooney (p. 383) is also referred to as Bram Guernsey (p. 333) It's possible that Cloke is friendly with two Brams, but given the relatively small number of named characters in the book, it seems that this is possibly an error?

12. "If on a Winter's Night a Reveller . . ." Part II, p. 20

13. Helen Bacon, *Virginia Quarterly Review* (1958), 276, cited in PG Walsh, Introduction to *The Satyricon* p. xxi

14. Edmund Wilson, *Axel's Castle* p. 100

15. Edmund Wilson, *Axel's Castle*, p. 106

16. Edmund Wilson, *Axel's Castle*, p. 124

17. *The Tragedy of Doctor Faustus* V (ii) l.123–4

18. *The Birth of Tragedy*, p. 8

19. *The Birth of Tragedy*, p. 7

20. Francois Pauw, "If on a Winter's Night a Reveller . . ." II, pp. 25–6

3. Reception of *The Secret History*

1. But if you *are* interested: Striped shirt and shorts from Gap Kids because she's tiny (5ft, 6½ stone), smokes Marlboro Gold but used to smoke Lucky Strikes.

2. Susannah Hunnewell in a profile of DT accompanying Andrew Rosenheim's *New York Times* Book Review: "Though she disagrees, Ms. Tartt says she is flattered when people think her novel is based to some extent on her life at Bennington. "There was this painter the Romans loved who painted grapes that looked so real that dogs would jump up and try to eat them off the walls. My duty as a writer is to fool you."

3. Nancy Wood "A Lethal Frenzy: Pagan Rites Go Wrong in a Compelling Novel" p. 85 *Macleans* October 12 1992 105:41 *Spy* had satirised the Brat Pack novel by producing a template, 'Novel-O-Matic'.

4. Star, *New Republic*

5. Wood, *London Review of Books*

6. Anita LeClerc and Joseph Hooper, "Tartt's Sweet Deal" *Esquire Magazine* p. 69 18:3 September 1992

7. Gary Krist, *Hudson Review* p. 241 46:1 Spring 1993

8. Barbara Melvin p. 53 See also Louis A Ruprecht Jr "Hellenism on Display" *Journal of Modern Greek Studies* 15:2 October 1997. Ruprecht footnotes *The Secret History* in an article otherwise concerned about the marginalisation of Classics in Universities.

4. The Novel's Performance

1. "Anatomy of a Hype" *Newsweek*

2. Interview with Ray Suarez, National Public Radio, 1997

3. Alexander Star *New Republic*

- Vanity Fair   1992
- Codehe article